THE ROYAL DRAGOON GUARDS

A REGIMENTAL HISTORY, 1685–2018

PETER MACFARLANE

FSC
www.fsc.org

MIX
Paper from
responsible sources
FSC® C014688

OSPREY PUBLISHING
Bloomsbury Publishing Plc
PO Box 883, Oxford, OX1 9PL, UK
1385 Broadway, 5th Floor, New York, NY 10018, USA
E-mail: info@ospreypublishing.com
www.ospreypublishing.com

OSPREY is a trademark of Osprey Publishing Ltd

First published in Great Britain in 2019

A catalogue record for this book is available from the British Library.

ISBN: PB 9781472838599; eBook 9781472838605;
ePDF 9781472838575; XML 9781472838582

19 20 21 22 23   10 9 8 7 6 5 4 3 2 1

Index by Zoe Ross

Page layout by Myriam Bell Design, Shrewsbury, UK

Originated by PDQ Digital Media Solutions, Bungay, UK

Printed in China through World Print Ltd.

Osprey Publishing supports the Woodland Trust, the UK's leading woodland conservation charity.

To find out more about our authors and books visit www.ospreypublishing.com. Here you will find extracts, author interviews, details of forthcoming events and the option to sign up for our newsletter.

FRONT COVER IMAGES:

Top: The charge of the Inniskilling Dragoons at the battle of Fontenoy, 11 May 1745, during the War of the Austrian Succession. (RDG)

Middle: Corporal Stenton of the Royal Dragoon Guards giving covering fire during the evacuation of a wounded British soldier in Helmand, Afghanistan, on 21 July 2010. Corporal Stenton was fatally injured in this action and was posthumously awarded the Military Cross for gallantry. (RDG)

Bottom right: Regimental cap badge. (UK Ministry of Defence © Crown Copyright)

BACK COVER IMAGES:

Top centre: C Squadron of the 4th/7th Royal Dragoon Guards moving up in the Reichswald, February 1945. (Imperial War Museum)

Top left: Cornet Richardson at the battle of Dettingen, 27 June 1743. (RDG)

Middle left: Regimental cap badge. (UK Ministry of Defence © Crown Copyright)

Bottom left: Detail from painting of the 5th Dragoon Guards capturing a German train at Harbonnières, 8th August 1918. (RDG)

TITLE PAGE IMAGE:

Sergeant Richards leading a strike operation by B Squadron of the Royal Dragoon Guards against insurgents in Basra in April 2008. Sergeant Richards was awarded the Military Cross for gallantry in this action. (RDG)

CONTENTS

FOREWORD

By Colonel N. C. T. Millen OBE
Colonel of the Regiment, The Royal Dragoon Guards

Regiments are living entities, and so with a change of role and a move planned for the coming years it seems a good time to reflect on the Regiment's heritage. This will further our understanding of how the Royal Dragoon Guards we know today has been shaped by its antecedent regiments, and what they have done, since they were raised over 300 years ago.

Colonel of the Regiment. (RDG)

Although our regimental history is already comprehensively covered in published books and numerous other documents, the whole story has never before been presented in such a concise and easily accessed format. With this book, those of us who have long since hung up our spurs, those still serving, and I hope those interested in joining can see how, in different times and circumstances and many places, our regiments have gone about their business. Our story is one of individual service and sacrifice, of triumph and disaster, and above all else of the comradeship that comes with the privilege of being a regimental soldier.

Whilst the story belongs to us all, the credit for presenting it here belongs to Lieutenant Colonel Peter Macfarlane. This book was Peter's vision and it is his passion for all matters regimental as well as his extraordinary commitment that made it happen. I thank him on behalf of us all.

INTRODUCTION

All four founding regiments were raised between 1685 and 1689 during the protracted contest between James II and William of Orange for the English throne.

'Arran's Horse' – the 4th Dragoon Guards – and 'Shrewsbury's Horse' – the 5th Dragoon Guards – were formed in 1685 from troops of horse raised by James to expand the army. Both regiments, together with the rest of James's army, refused to support him against William of Orange and in 1688 he abandoned the throne and fled to France. William immediately raised a number of new regiments including 'Devonshire's Horse' – the 7th Dragoon Guards.

The following year, still claiming the throne, James landed in Ireland. Only Londonderry and Enniskillen resisted, both held by garrisons of refugees loyal to William. At Enniskillen the refugees elected officers and 'formed themselves into a strong body of Horse with an adjunct of Foot'. These were formally established in 1690 and included 'Conyingham's Dragoons' – the 6th (Inniskilling) Dragoons. William landed in Ireland in the same year with an army that included the 5th and 7th and all three regiments fought at the Boyne.

The 4th and 5th also accompanied William to the Low Countries to confront Louis XIV in the War of the Grand Alliance, the first of many British campaigns in north-west Europe. The peace that followed was short-lived and the War of the Spanish Succession broke out in 1702. The 5th and the 7th campaigned under Marlborough and participated in all his major actions. After the Treaty of Utrecht in 1713 they joined the 4th in Ireland. The Inniskillings spent much of the century in Britain and were involved in suppressing the first Jacobite Rebellion in 1715. Both the Inniskillings and the 7th also served in the War of the Austrian Succession and the Seven Years' War.

Meanwhile, the 4th and the 5th languished in Ireland where they accumulated some 180 years of joint service. They were joined for lengthy

---

Commission for raising Devonshire's Horse

We, reposing especial faith and confidence in your fidelity, courage and good conduct, do by these presents constitute and appoint you to be Colonel of a regiment of Horse to be forthwith raised for our service, and likewise to be a Captain of a troop in the same regiment. You are therefore to take the said regiment as colonel, and the said troop as captain, into your care and charge, and duly to exercise as the officers as soldiers thereof in arms; and to use your best endeavours to keep them in good order and discipline. And We hereby command them to obey you as their Colonel and Captain respectively. And you are to observe and follow such orders and directions, from time to time, as you shall receive from Us, or any, your superior Officer, according to the rules and discipline of War, in pursuance of the trust We repose in you.

Dated ye 31st December 1688

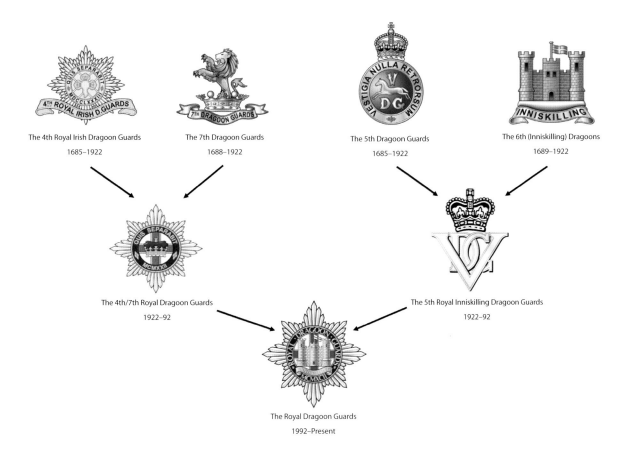

The 4th Royal Irish Dragoon Guards
1685–1922

The 7th Dragoon Guards
1688–1922

The 5th Dragoon Guards
1685–1922

The 6th (Inniskilling) Dragoons
1689–1922

The 4th/7th Royal Dragoon Guards
1922–92

The 5th Royal Inniskilling Dragoon Guards
1922–92

The Royal Dragoon Guards
1992–Present

The antecedent regiments of the Royal Dragoon Guards. (UK Ministry of Defence © Crown Copyright)

spells by the 7th, endured a monotonous routine of mounted constabulary tasks, and sank into a low state of effectiveness and discipline. Another war with France in 1793 briefly took the 5th to the Low Countries with the Inniskillings. They returned to Ireland in time to join the 4th and 7th in crushing a French-backed rebellion in 1798.

Napoleon was thwarted in his plans to invade Britain in 1805, but two years later he turned his attention to the Iberian Peninsula, occupying Portugal and forcing the evacuation of a British expeditionary force in 1809. Later that year the future Duke of Wellington returned to Portugal with another expeditionary force and began the campaign that culminated five years later in France. The 4th and 5th joined him in 1811 and the Inniskillings took part in Napoleon's final defeat at Waterloo in 1815.

For the next 30 years all four regiments spent much of their service on garrison duty, which included aid to the civil power. The 7th also saw active service in southern Africa in the 1840s, in a foretaste of future campaigns on that continent.

By 1854 the army had suffered years of neglect and none of the 4th, 5th or Inniskillings were in good shape for what they would encounter in the Crimea. They nonetheless acquitted themselves with distinction at Balaklava.

From 1858 onwards each regiment had extended spells of service in India. The Inniskillings served in South Africa, the 4th and 7th campaigned

Inniskilling Dragoons on manoeuvres by a ruined house, c.1870. (RDG)

in Egypt and detachments of the 4th and 5th fought in Sudan. At the turn of the century the 5th, 7th and Inniskillings took part in the Boer War in South Africa.

Following an early phase of mounted operations at the start of the First World War, during which the 4th and 5th played leading roles, all four regiments were primarily committed to trench warfare on the Western Front. The end of the war brought regimental amalgamations and in 1922 the 4th and the 7th merged, as did the 5th and the Inniskillings. The two new regiments remained as mounted cavalry until 1938 when mechanisation began. Both regiments went to France at the outbreak of the Second World War in 1939, equipped with rudimentary light reconnaissance tanks.

Following the Dunkirk evacuation in 1940, both regiments spent four frustrating years in Britain waiting for active service. The opportunity finally

Regimental Titles

In 1922 the 4th and the 7th Dragoon Guards merged to become the 4th/7th Dragoon Guards. The Royal title was granted in 1936. The 5th Dragoon Guards and 6th (Inniskilling) Dragoons merged to form the 5th/6th Dragoons in 1922. They became the 5th Inniskilling Dragoon Guards in 1927 and the Royal title was granted in 1935. The regiment was widely known as 'the Skins'.

arrived in 1944 with the Allied landings in Normandy, in which the 4th/7th played a prominent part, followed by the campaign through France and the Low Countries, and into Germany.

The 'Cold War' between the West and the Soviet Union began shortly after the end of the Second World War. Both regiments spent many years in West Germany confronting the Warsaw Pact powers. They were also called on for a variety of tasks in support of Britain's interests in both the Middle East and Far East. The 4th/7th served in Palestine, the Skins fought in Korea against Chinese and North Korean communist forces, and both regiments saw active service in South Arabia and kept the peace in Cyprus. Nearer to home, Northern Ireland also made its demands.

Cavalry regiments did not have formal recruiting areas until 1958, when the 4th/7th were allotted North and West Yorkshire and the Skins were allotted Northern Ireland. The Skins subsequently added Cumberland and Westmoreland (latterly Cumbria) and Cheshire. These links were reinforced by the opening of regimental home headquarters and territorial affiliations with yeomanry regiments, including the Queen's Own Yorkshire Yeomanry, the North Irish Horse and the Cheshire Yeomanry.

The end of the Cold War in 1989 again saw reductions in the army. In 1992 the 4th/7th and Skins, who had a strong shared history, amalgamated in Germany to form the Royal Dragoon Guards. The territorial links with Yorkshire and Northern Ireland were retained and the regiment was granted the Freedom of York in 1999. The Skins had previously been granted the Freedom of Enniskillen in 1956.

The turn of the century saw a new range of operational demands, with the regiment seeing active service in Northern Ireland, Bosnia, Iraq and Afghanistan. More recently, soldiers from the regiment have deployed to support the national armies of Ukraine, Estonia and Latvia.

Now designated an armoured cavalry regiment, the Royal Dragoon Guards provides reconnaissance at the brigade and division levels.

A Challenger 2 main battle tank of A Squadron of the Royal Dragoon Guards, Iraq, Operation TELIC 5. (RDG)

CHAPTER ONE – REGIMENTAL LIFE

ROLES

There were originally two types of British cavalry – horse and dragoons. The latter were soldiers who dismounted to fight with the musket, rather than fighting from horseback. The distinctions between dragoons and the rest of the cavalry became blurred and by the end of Marlborough's era had largely disappeared. From the middle of the 18th century the old regiments of horse began to be converted to dragoons as part of an economy measure to save money on both horses and pay. They were given the title 'dragoon guards' to cushion their pride and, along with dragoons, were categorised as heavy cavalry with the primary role of breaking the enemy using shock action.

ORGANISATION

Until 1892 the troop was the standard subunit in a cavalry regiment. Troops were 50 to 60 strong and led by a captain, supported by a lieutenant, cornet (2nd lieutenant) and troop sergeant-major. Establishments varied but regiments had up to eight troops until after the Napoleonic Wars, when they were reduced to six. On active service two troops would form the regimental depot at home, while the remainder formed the fighting troops. These would be grouped into squadrons, each usually comprising two troops led by the senior captain.

TRAINING

Training in the early mounted era was rudimentary and primarily concentrated on learning how to ride, use a sword and carbine, and carry out a series of drills. Collective training was infrequent and took the form of field days, which were often a set of drills undertaken to satisfy an inspecting officer. A further bar to efficient training was imposed by constant changes

Soldiers of the 4th Dragoon Guards on fatigue duties at Tidworth, 1912. (RDG)

of station. The 5th Dragoon Guards moved between Ireland and England eight times in 33 years, and between 1817 and 1854 their regimental headquarters was stationed in more than 50 locations.

The lessons learnt from the Boer War led to significant and wide-ranging improvements in both individual and collective training. Skill at arms became increasingly important, with pay linked to proficiency on the range, and in 1912 the 6th (Inniskilling) Dragoons were placed third in an army-wide shooting competition. The onset of mechanisation led to the development of

A detachment of the 5th Dragoon Guards at Athy, Co. Kildare, on the line of march from the Curragh (the Salisbury Plain of Ireland), June 1865. (RDG)

Farrier sergeants of the 5th Dragoon Guards at York, 1872. (RDG)

Families of the 7th Dragoon Guards in Egypt, 1893. (RDG)

trade training and career courses, together with progressive and structured collective and all arms training. From the 1960s adventurous training gave young officers and NCOs the opportunities to develop leadership skills during expeditions that were often conducted in remote parts of the world.

CAMPAIGNING

Until the 20th century, campaigning in Europe followed a set pattern dictated by the seasons. During the winter, roads would often become impassable and little pasture would be available for horse fodder. Armies, therefore, usually manoeuvred and fought during the summer and autumn. Following the harvest they built up their supplies of grain and fodder and went into winter quarters. Once the weather improved and pasturage became available they would take to the field again.

HOME SERVICE
Aid to the Civil Power

Before police forces existed the army was widely employed on constabulary duties and was the first line of response to disturbances, particularly industrial unrest. In 1808 the 4th Dragoon Guards quelled a serious riot by Manchester

weavers and in 1810 it put down outbreaks of rioting in the mining areas of Durham and Northumberland.

Modern-day aid to the civil power has included manning fire engines during fire brigade strikes, most recently in the winter of 2002 when the Royal Dragoon Guards were deployed on Operation FRESCO. In an earlier example of troops acting as firemen, four troops of the 7th Dragoon Guards, with their barracks fire engine, responded to a major fire at York Minster in 1829.

The last mounted parade of the 4th/7th Royal Dragoon Guards, Edinburgh, 1938. (RDG)

4th/7th Royal Dragoon Guards firefighting crews during Operation BRAVADO in Belfast, 1977–78. (R. Griffin)

Billets and Barracks

Regiments were widely dispersed, especially in Ireland, and it was extremely rare for a regiment to be assembled in one place. It was also common for troops to be split up into even smaller detachments. There were few barracks until the late 19th century and the small numbers that existed rarely accommodated more than a troop. In England billeting in public houses and inns was the norm, while in Scotland and Ireland soldiers could also be billeted in private houses.

MUSIC AND SPORT
Bands

The regimental bands made an important contribution to regimental life and morale until their merger into what is now the the Band of the Royal Armoured Corps. The Quick March of the Royal Dragoon Guards, 'Fare Thee Well Enniskillen', is inherited from the 5th Royal Inniskilling Dragoon Guards; 'Inseparable', the Slow March, came from the 4th/7th Royal Dragoon Guards.

Musicians from both regiments deployed in the 1991 Gulf War as medical orderlies and bandsmen. The Royal Dragoon Guards today has its own established Pipes and Drums, reflecting its Irish traditions inherited from the 4th Royal Irish Dragoon Guards and the Skins.

Sport

From the late Victorian era sport became an important aspect of regimental life and an increasingly important requirement for morale and regimental pride.

The Cavalry Cup for soccer was instituted in 1896 and one or other of the regiments has often been triumphant. For example, the 4th/7th and Skins were winners four times between 1933 and 1938 and the Royal Dragoon Guards were victorious in 2012 and 2017.

Trooper Smith of the 5th Inniskilling Dragoon Guards Musical Ride, York, 1929. The 5th Inniskilling Dragoon Guards Musical Ride was an equitation display team of 30 horses and riders in full dress uniform, supported by the Regimental Band. In a half-hour performance, each horse and rider made 128 jumps. The Trick Ride performed stunts including vaulting and jumping over varied and unusual obstacles. Both rides performed at horse and country shows and military tattoos from 1929 to 1938. (RDG)

Cricket was also widely played from the late Victorian era onwards. The Skins won the Cavalry Cup three years running between 1989 and 1991, as well as the Army Cup in 1990. The Royal Dragoon Guards continued this run of success as British Army (Germany) champions from 1993 to 1995.

Post-war service in Germany offered access to skiing, with Exercise SNOW QUEEN in Bavaria becoming an annual feature of the calendar, along with downhill, slalom and langlauf championships. Captain Legard of the Skins competed in the Winter Olympics in 1936 in the Combined Nordic event. Lieutenant Woodall of the 4th/7th competed in the luge in 1972 and 1976.

The years in India and South Africa gave ample opportunity for polo, still played by the Royal Dragoon Guards today. The Inniskillings won the Delhi Durbar Cup in 1911 and Captain Ritson captained the England polo team in 1913. The 4th and 5th Dragoon Guards both won the Inter-Regimental Cup several times in South Africa and Britain.

The Skins had a strong record in the modern pentathlon, winning the British national team championships four times between 1947 and 1951. Lieutenant Duckworth and Lance Corporal Martin each also won the individual championship twice. Captain Legard competed in the Olympics in 1932 and 1936 and Sergeant Bright coached the 1976 Olympic Gold medal winners.

The 5th Royal Inniskilling Dragoon Guards celebrate having beaten the Royal Scots Greys 1-0 in the Cavalry Cup Final, 1936. The team captain, Lance Corporal (later Sergeant) Workman, holding the cups aloft, was killed in action at Dunkirk in May 1940. (TopFoto.co.uk)

Polar Exploration

The Royal Dragoon Guards have a unique connection with Polar exploration. In 1910 Captain Oates of the Inniskillings volunteered to look after the ponies on Captain Scott's second expedition to the South Pole. In doing so, Oates became the first soldier to reach Antarctica and the South Pole.

Having reached the South Pole in January 1912, Scott's party encountered unseasonably harsh weather on the return journey. Temperatures plunged to minus 40°C and Oates was afflicted by severe frostbite. On 17 March 1912

In the footsteps of a legend: the Royal Dragoon Guards expedition to the South Pole 2012–13. (RDG)

– St Patrick's Day, and also his birthday – realising that he was a grave hindrance to the chances of survival of his comrades, he said to Scott: 'I am going outside and may be some time.' He walked out of the tent into a raging blizzard and was never seen again. Scott wrote in his diary, 'He was a very gallant gentleman', and the manner of his sacrifice entered British history.

On the Sunday nearest to St Patrick's Day the Royal Dragoon Guards holds an annual Church Parade to commemorate Oates' sacrifice and example. The regiment is unique in the British Army in honouring an individual in this manner. The link with Oates is also retained through a regimental tradition of Polar expeditions. In 2012 four members of the regiment took part in an expedition to the South Pole that retraced the route taken by Oates on his fateful journey a century before.

CHAPTER TWO – KEEPING THE PEACE

The history of all the parent regiments is interspersed with spells of peacekeeping and maintaining law and order. These most often occurred in Ireland, but also in India and the Middle East, particularly during Britain's withdrawal from the Empire after 1945.

INDIA, 1857–1928

All the parent regiments served at least one tour in India from the late 1850s, generally without incident. The 4th Dragoon Guards saw active service against Afridi tribesmen on the North-West Frontier in 1897, providing escorts and undertaking patrols in sweltering heat.

Camp of the 4th Dragoon Guards near the Khyber Pass at Jamrud (now Pakistan), 1897. (Courtesy of the Council of the National Army Museum, London)

A Cromwell tank and Bren Gun carriers of the 4th/7th Royal Dragoon Guards on a show of force in central Tel Aviv, 1947. This was the first time British tanks had entered the city and Jewish protestors responded with petrol bombs. (RDG)

After the Indian Mutiny of 1857 each British regiment was brigaded with two Indian regiments, ensuring a core of British troops in every garrison. Cavalry brigades were named after their garrison towns, and the Royal Dragoon Guards' affiliation with the Deccan Horse dates from the 7th Dragoon Guards' service in the Secunderabad Brigade from 1910 to 1918, including three years on the Western Front.

PALESTINE, 1938–48

After the First World War Britain was awarded a mandate to govern Palestine. Its pledge to support the establishment of a Jewish homeland led to an uprising by Palestinian Arabs in 1936. In 1938 the 4th/7th Royal Dragoon Guards and the 5th Royal Inniskilling Dragoon Guards each sent a motorised squadron to reinforce the horsed cavalry regiments in Palestine. Their tasks included escorts, patrols, searches, raids and supporting the police. These internal security tasks would feature in many subsequent campaigns.

After the Second World War Jewish terrorist groups, including the Irgun and the Stern Gang, sought the destruction of the British Mandate and the ejection of the Arab population. British troops, including the 4th/7th, became the target of a vicious terrorist campaign from 1946 to 1948. The 4th/7th's tasks included searches, checkpoints, patrols and manning observation posts, and three soldiers were killed in action. One of their most distasteful tasks was escorting illegal Jewish immigrants, survivors of Hitler's death camps, to be deported. The regiment withdrew in 1948, when the British Mandate ended and the state of Israel was founded.

SUEZ CANAL ZONE, 1951–53

Britain maintained a military presence in Egypt to protect the Suez Canal under the terms of a treaty signed in 1936. Egyptian nationalists increasingly resented the British presence and, following riots in 1945, British troops withdrew to what became known as the Canal Zone. In October 1951 further rioting, arson and looting erupted along the canal. The 4th/7th's reconnaissance troop was deployed to reinforce the British garrison and spent three months patrolling the canal in scout cars in search of snipers and saboteurs. It came under small-arms fire an average of four nights a week, returning fire with machine guns and light mortars. Despite its vehicles being hit several times, the troop suffered no casualties. The Skins were stationed in the Canal Zone in 1953 on their return from Korea. The internal security situation deteriorated during the year, resulting in a heavy burden of guard duties and severe restrictions on movement, particularly at night.

SOUTH ARABIA, 1964–66

The final years of British rule in Aden and its hinterland, the Aden Protectorate, were marked by an Egyptian-backed insurgency and terrorist campaign resulting in a state of emergency being declared in 1965. The Skins, less C Squadron, were stationed in Aden from 1964 to 1965 as the internal security situation deteriorated and service families and military convoys were targeted. Reconnaissance Troop provided convoy escorts and patrols up country in the rugged and mountainous Radfan, in terrain and temperatures no less hostile than the dissident tribesmen. One soldier was seriously wounded in a mine strike.

The 4th/7th also saw active service in South Arabia from 1965 to 1966. Squadrons were deployed across the protectorate and along the Yemen border with troops deployed in widely dispersed locations. They faced threats from rockets, mines, grenades and small arms and saw frequent action in nearly one hundred separate engagements. One soldier was killed in a vehicle

Sergeant Binks of the 4th/7th Royal Dragoon Guards in a Saladin armoured car repelling an enemy rocket and small arms attack at Al Milah, South Arabia, 10 March 1966. He was subsequently awarded the Military Medal for his coolness under fire in this and a series of other actions. (RDG)

Ferret scout cars of the 5th Royal Inniskilling Dragoon Guards on UN peacekeeping operations in Cyprus, late 1960s. (Imperial War Museum)

accident and 20 were wounded in action. The regimental air troop played an important role in providing surveillance, casualty evacuation and urgent resupply. Squadrons also rotated through internal security tasks in Aden as the situation became increasingly fragile following the announcement that independence would be granted in 1968.

CYPRUS, 1966–88

Fighting between the Greek and Turkish populations led to the deployment of a United Nations peacekeeping force (UNFICYP) in 1964. Both regiments periodically provided squadrons in the reconnaissance role for UNFICYP tours and completed regimental tours in the dismounted role in the 1970s and 1980s. In 1966–67, A Squadron of the Skins was deployed at a time of high tensions and faced deliberate forest fires, demonstrations, communal violence and attempts to overrun UN positions. C Squadron of the 4th/7th was caught in the crossfire of the Turkish invasion of the island in 1974. Its patrols were frequently under shelling and air strikes and were fortunate not to suffer fatalities.

LIBYA, 1967

The Skins, less A Squadron, which was deployed in Cyprus with the UN, were stationed in Libya from 1966 to 1967 as part of the British garrison. Violent rioting broke out in Benghazi on 5 June 1967 at the start of the Six Day War between Arab nations and Israel. Mobs threatened the British and United States consulates and civilians, resulting in the deployment of riot squads from B and C squadrons with the air troop providing surveillance. Three soldiers were badly burned when the C Squadron command vehicle was set on fire by a mob. Internal security tasks continued for several weeks until the situation was stabilised.

Soldiers of C Squadron of the 4th/7th Royal Dragoon Guards in a lull between patrols, Belfast, 1972. (RDG)

NORTHERN IRELAND, 1972–99

In 1969 widespread civil disorder broke out in Northern Ireland leading to the deployment of British troops on Operation BANNER. It would become the longest continuous campaign in the army's history.

The 4th/7th carried out three squadron tours between 1972 and 1976 at the height of the Provisional Irish Republican Army's (PIRA) terrorist campaign. Their tasks included riot control, mounted reconnaissance, foot patrols, checkpoints and searches for weapons and explosives. One 4th/7th soldier was killed in 1972 and a Skins recruiting sergeant was murdered in 1974 while off duty.

From the late 1970s the army's role was increasingly to support the police. Irish regiments were excluded from Operation BANNER until 1981 when the Skins served in Fermanagh, the first Irish regiment to do so. The regiment deployed again in 1989/90. Both regiments also provided squadrons as the guard force for the Maze prison, and individuals also served as staff officers and in aviation and specialist units.

Soldiers of A Squadron of the 5th Royal Inniskilling Dragoon Guards on foot patrol in Londonderry, 1989. (RDG)

The Royal Dragoon Guards deployed twice during the 1990s, during the delicate steps towards the end of the conflict. PIRA still posed a dangerous and sophisticated threat and the army was also increasingly deployed to maintain public order against violent loyalist protests. The 1998 Good Friday Agreement did much to resolve political differences between loyalists and nationalists. PIRA declared an end to its armed campaign in 2005 and Operation BANNER ended in 2007 when responsibility for security passed to the police.

BOSNIA, 1997–98

The end of the Cold War led to Yugoslavia fracturing into its constituent elements and a brutal civil war in Bosnia between three factions – Muslims, Serbs and Croats. The civil war was ended by the Dayton Peace Agreement in December 1995 and NATO forces deployed to enforce the fragile peace. In 1997–98 A Squadron of the Royal Dragoon Guards served in Bosnia, conducting mobile and dismounted patrols and providing an armoured deterrent.

CHAPTER THREE – SMALL WARS

Throughout its history the British Army has fought against insurgents and irregular enemies, mainly in Africa and the Middle East, but also occasionally in the British Isles against nationalist rebels. In the Victorian era these became known as 'small wars' to distinguish them from the major wars between regular armies in Europe. 'Small' was a relative expression – the area over which operations were conducted in South Africa between 1899 and 1902 was as large as France and Germany combined. The parent regiments faced determined foes and hostile climates and terrain that made 'small war' soldiering as demanding as any in their history.

JACOBITE REBELLIONS, 1715 AND 1745

Scots supporters of the Old Pretender, James Stuart, rebelled in 1715. The 6th (Inniskilling) Dragoons formed part of a small force that confronted a rebel army at Sheriffmuir. Both sides claimed victory after an indecisive battle in which the Inniskillings helped to rout the rebels' right wing. However, the Jacobite rebels failed to close in on the weakened government force and withdrew to Perth.

Another Jacobite rising took place in 1745 in support of the Young Pretender, Charles Stuart. The Jacobite army marched as far south as Derby before Charles lost his nerve and turned for home. The government troops pursuing them included four troops of the 7th Dragoon Guards, who took part in a dismounted skirmish with the rebel rearguard at Clifton Moor.

IRELAND, 1798

Ireland was frequently torn by strife, with potential for disturbance from religious intolerance or nationalism. The 4th, 5th and 7th Dragoon Guards were involved in suppressing a major French-backed rebellion by the United Irishmen in 1798. The 4th and the 5th took part in the one-sided battle of Vinegar Hill, and the 5th helped compel the surrender of a French force in Mayo.

SOUTH AFRICA, 1845–47

The 7th served in South Africa from 1843 to 1847 as part of the garrison of Cape Colony. In 1845 five troops were sent to suppress dissident Dutch settlers, known as Boers, who were raiding Cape territory. In a brief campaign a Boer stronghold was overrun without loss and many Boers subsequently laid down their arms.

The 7th Dragoon Guards charging at the Gwanga River in South Africa, 8 June 1846. The battle was over in just ten minutes. (RDG)

In 1846 the regiment took part in bush warfare in Kaffirland following the breakdown of relations between the Cape authorities and the Kaffir tribes. It was a campaign of skirmishes, ambushes and long marches and counter-marches, a foretaste of future wars in Africa. Bringing the enemy to action was the hardest task. One of the rare occasions on which this was accomplished was at the Gwanga River, when a squadron routed a body of tribesmen caught in the open.

EGYPT AND SUDAN, 1882–85

In 1882 a nationalist uprising in Egypt led by Arabi Pasha threatened the route to India through the recently constructed Suez Canal. A force of 40,000 British and Indian troops, including the 4th (reinforced by 78 soldiers from the 5th) and 7th, was dispatched under General Wolseley. Both regiments disembarked unopposed at Ismailia in August and were immediately involved in successful actions to secure the canal. General Wolseley then planned a surprise attack against Arabi Pasha's 60,000-strong army at Tel-el-Kebir on the road to Cairo. A bold night approach was followed by a successful dawn attack on 12 September, which defeated the Egyptians in 35 minutes. The British and Indian cavalry completed the rout, with neither the 4th nor 7th suffering a single casualty. Cairo fell the following day, with the 4th being the first British troops to enter the capital where they captured Arabi Pasha's personal standard. The war had lasted less than a month and was notable for its excellent planning and administration and few British casualties.

The 7th Dragoon Guards at the Sphinx after the occupation of Cairo, 1882. (RDG)

Two years later General Gordon was besieged in Khartoum by a Dervish chief who had proclaimed himself as Mahdi (Messiah) and revolted against Egyptian rule. A relief operation, which included a specially raised composite Camel Corps, was mounted. The 4th and 5th both provided detachments of 45 soldiers as part of this corps. The force reached Korti, some 900 miles up the Nile from Cairo, by boat on Christmas Day 1884. It then divided into a river column and a desert column. On 17 January 1885 the desert column, 1,800 strong and including the Camel Corps, was confronted by a horde of over 9,000 Mahdi fanatics close to the wells of Abu Klea. With the need for water pressing, a large dismounted square was formed to advance to the wells. A savage and bloody close-quarter battle followed, in which the square finally reached the wells having broken the Mahdist attacks and despite suffering severe losses. The detachments of the 4th and 5th lost over a third of their strength, including both commanders killed. The column pushed on towards a loop in the Nile to meet the river column, fighting another less-costly battle just before reaching the river. There it was learned that Khartoum had fallen and Gordon was dead. The Sudan was abandoned and the expeditionary force evacuated. Despite their casualties and share of the fighting, the 4th and 5th did not qualify for the award of Abu Klea as a battle honour as they had only been present in detachment rather than squadron or regimental strength.

The Battle of Abu Klea, 17 January 1885. The detachments of the 4th and 5th Dragoon Guards formed part of the near side of the square, the scene of the heaviest fighting. (Courtesy of the Council of the National Army Museum, London)

SOUTH AFRICA, 1881–1902

From 1880 to 1881 there was a brief war between Britain and the Boer settlers of the Transvaal, in which the latter secured their independence. The Inniskillings were warned for active service and sailed for South Africa, but arrived after an armistice had been signed. The regiment subsequently took part in an expedition to Bechuanaland in 1884 to enforce British rights against enclaves of Boer freebooters. The territories were restored to British rule without a shot being fired.

War broke out again in 1899 between Britain and the Boer republics of the Transvaal and the Orange Free State. The 5th, reinforced by 18 soldiers from the 4th, arrived in Natal in October, just as hostilities opened. The regiment immediately moved by rail to Ladysmith, where British troops were concentrating to meet the Boer invasion of Natal.

On 21 October a small force, including D Squadron of the 5th, clashed with a Boer force at Elandslaagte. Sergeant Taylor wrote: 'We had…our first taste of Mauser [the German rifle used by the Boers]; we now for the first time heard the screech and thud of the shell.' An assault by infantry and dismounted yeomanry forced the Boers to retreat, giving D Squadron the opportunity to charge and rout the fleeing enemy. Only the onset of darkness saved the

Soldiers of the 5th Dragoon Guards manning fortified sangars during the siege of Ladysmith. (RDG)

The Inniskilling Dragoons crossing the Liebenberg Vlei in the Orange River Colony during one of the endless column operations of the Boer War. (RDG)

Boers from complete destruction. It was the sole example of a profitable cavalry charge during the war.

Another action near Ladysmith on 30 October led to a severe British reverse. The 5th only had a few soldiers wounded, including Private Mouncer of D Squadron who was hit and fell from his horse while withdrawing. Lieutenant Norwood galloped back under heavy fire, dismounted, and picking up Mouncer, carried him out of fire on his back while leading his horse with one hand. Norwood was awarded the Victoria Cross.

The Boers, superior in marksmanship, fieldcraft and tactics, now had the initiative. The British force at Ladysmith, including the 5th, found itself under siege, along with other garrisons at Mafeking and Kimberley. The supply situation was precarious and sickness and disease ravaged the weakened troops. A series of uncoordinated attempts to relieve all three garrisons met with disastrous setbacks, casting gloom and a sense of uncertainty across the army and in Britain.

The army was reorganised in January 1900 under the command of Field Marshal Roberts. From the outset, he determined to take the offensive by directly threatening the Boer capitals of Bloemfontein and Pretoria. This would force the Boers to fight on the defensive and withdraw some of the forces besieging the British troops.

The Inniskillings disembarked at Cape Town in November 1899 and joined the forces concentrating on the border between the Cape Colony and the

Lieutenant Norwood of the 5th Dragoon Guards rescuing Private Mouncer near Ladysmith on 30 October 1899. Norwood was awarded the Victoria Cross for this action. (RDG)

Orange Free State. In February 1900 A Squadron joined the cavalry division, which made a spectacular outflanking march to relieve Kimberley, although at a substantial cost in horses. The squadron then helped to cut the railway north of Bloemfontein, leading to the city's fall. The rest of the regiment remained on the border as part of a force holding down several thousand Boers. After the capture of Bloemfontein, the advance paused and the Inniskillings were reunited. Mafeking was relieved in May. Its defence, conducted by Colonel Baden-Powell (late of the 5th), had excited widespread public admiration at a time of gloom over earlier defeats.

The siege of Ladysmith was lifted at the end of February. An attempt to pursue the retreating Boers was made by the one squadron of the 5th that could be mounted, but the horses were so weak they could not sustain the effort. Following Ladysmith, the 5th were reconstituted before spending the next 15 months securing the lines of communication in northern Natal.

The 7th disembarked at Cape Town in March 1900 and took part, with the Inniskillings, in the advance on Pretoria. This involved lengthy marches interspersed with sharp fighting. Pretoria surrendered in early June, marking the end of organised Boer resistance. The 7th took part in one of the last major set-piece battles of the war, at Diamond Hill on 11–12 June, suffering only five wounded in spite of being pinned down for two days under intense fire.

Inniskilling Dragoons officers' mess shelter, South Africa. (RDG)

The Siege of Ladysmith

The ration at this time [January 1900] was: preserved meat, ½ lb, or fresh meat, 1 lb; biscuits, ½ lb, or 1 lb bread; tea or coffee, 1⅙ oz; sugar, 1½ oz; salt, ½ oz; pepper, 1/36 oz. It does not read, however, as bad as it tasted. The bread was bread in name only. It was believed to be made almost entirely of oats and violet powder, mixed with a little rye; anyway, that is what it tasted like. The fresh meat was either horse or trek-ox, and even the vigorous found it difficult to get their teeth through it. The preserved meat existed only in imagination; at least none of it ever came the way of the 5th Dragoon Guards. The pepper and salt were of good quality, but did not in themselves form a very satisfying ration.[1]

1 Pomeroy, Maj R. L., *History of the Fifth Dragoon Guards*, Blackwood, Edinburgh (1924), Vol 1, p249.

The Boer leadership, however, refused to surrender. Nearly two years of guerrilla warfare followed, which involved the 5th, 7th and Inniskillings in hard, exhausting, often dangerous and sometimes distasteful operations. Independent Boer commandos ambushed convoys, sabotaged railways, raided towns and proved themselves to be formidable opponents, able to strike swiftly and melt away into the wide expanses of open grassland known as the veldt.

To counter the Boers the veldt was divided into areas allocated to mobile columns to patrol. Blockhouses were built along railways, providing bases for columns to pivot on. The cavalry exchanged carbines and swords for rifles and bayonets. Extended sweeps and marches took place, involving minor actions and skirmishes. On one march in October 1900 the Inniskillings were nearly surrounded by a force of Boers, losing eight killed and 27 wounded. What became known as the Ermelo March went on for ten days with fighting all the way. Between April and June 1901 the 7th trekked continuously for nine weeks, covering nearly 1,500 miles. Thousands of horses, cattle and other livestock and hundreds of carts were seized, but fewer than 150 Boers were killed or captured. The regiment lost two soldiers killed and seven wounded.

The Boers finally surrendered in May 1902. The war had cost the three regiments nearly 200 fatalities between them. Some were killed in action or died from wounds, but many died from disease and sickness. Many valuable lessons were learned.

MESOPOTAMIA, 1920–21

At the end of the First World War Britain was awarded a mandate to govern Mesopotamia (modern Iraq). In 1920 an armed uprising by Shia tribes on the middle and lower Euphrates threatened British rule, with isolated garrisons besieged and relief columns attacked. Thousands of British and Indian troops, including the 7th, were used to suppress the insurrection. The regiment carried out punitive raids, chased rebel bands and suffered badly from sandfly fever and heat exhaustion in the harsh climate.

Battle Honours – Small Wars

4th Dragoon Guards
  Tel-el-Kebir
  Egypt 1882
5th Dragoon Guards
  Defence of Ladysmith
  South Africa 1899–1902
7th Dragoon Guards
  South Africa 1846–47
  Tel-el-Kebir
  Egypt 1882
  South Africa 1900–02
6th (Inniskilling) Dragoons
  South Africa 1899–1902

CHAPTER FOUR – MAJOR WARS OF THE 17TH CENTURY

WILLIAMITE WAR IN IRELAND, 1688–91

In 1688 King James II fled to France and Prince William of Orange became King. The 4th and 5th Dragoon Guards joined the rest of the army in switching allegiance to William and were soon reinforced by newly raised regiments, including the 7th Dragoon Guards.

James landed in Ireland with French troops the following year in an attempt to regain his throne. One of the few places to resist him was Enniskillen, where the population remained loyal to William and raised irregular regiments to defend the town. In 1690, following successful actions against larger rebel forces at Newtownbutler and Lisnaskea, they were established as regular regiments, including the 6th (Inniskilling) Dragoons. Their staunch resistance enabled William to send reinforcements, including the 5th and the 7th, from England.

All three regiments fought under William's command at the Boyne on 1 July 1690, with four troops of Inniskillings forming part of William's personal escort. This was a dangerous role, as the King personally led his cavalry across the river under fire from close range, rallying his troops as they charged and counter-charged. The day ended with James's forces driven from the field in disorder.

The Inniskilling Dragoons crossing the Boyne, 1 July 1690. (RDG)

The Boyne decided the war but did not end it. James fled back to France but his Irish supporters fought on. The decisive battle was fought a year later at Aughrim, where the Inniskillings seized an important pass. This was followed by disaster a few weeks later when they were surprised by a dawn raid on their camp near Sligo. The survivors scattered with the loss of tents, baggage and supplies.

WAR OF THE GRAND ALLIANCE, 1691–97

For William the campaign in Ireland had been a diversion from the greater menace faced from France, the most powerful state in Europe. In 1692 he took to the field in command of the Grand Alliance, which aimed to keep King Louis XIV out of the Low Countries. His forces included the 4th, 5th and 7th, taking part in the first of their many campaigns in Continental Europe. They and their successors were to become very familiar with the terrain of north-west Europe over the next three hundred years.

In a war of protracted manoeuvres and lengthy sieges of well-fortified towns, the cavalry had little opportunity for action. An exception was the defeat at Landen in 1693, in which William led his cavalry in repeated charges to cover the withdrawal of the hard-pressed infantry. In the final charge the 4th helped to break the French *Maison du Roi* (household cavalry). The 4th's colonel, charging at the head of his regiment, was wounded and taken prisoner, but two months later was back in command having been exchanged for two French officers.

The war ended in stalemate. Despite the frustrations of the campaign the 4th, 5th and 7th were now veteran soldiers, experienced in the routines of active service and familiar with place names that were to have great significance to their successors: Mons, Ypres, Cambrai, Lessines and many more.

CHAPTER FIVE – MAJOR WARS OF THE 18TH CENTURY

The 18th century saw Britain fight a series of wars to prevent France becoming the dominant power in Europe. The main theatre of combat was the Low Countries and northern Germany, with fighting at times spilling over into northern France.

WAR OF THE SPANISH SUCCESSION, 1702–13

In 1702 the 5th and 7th Dragoon Guards formed part of the Duke of Marlborough's Anglo-Dutch army facing France in the Low Countries. The first two years of campaigning followed the familiar dreary round of siege operations and inconclusive manoeuvring. As 1704 opened, however, Bavaria allied itself with France and threatened the allied capital of Vienna. Marlborough therefore marched his army deep into Germany to join his

Austrian ally on the Danube and confront the French armies and their Bavarian allies. Careful logistic planning and deception were central to his plan. Captain Pope of the 7th wrote on 4 May:

> We marched in full order, all in good spirits to be on the move, making for the Meuse where tis said we meet with my Lord Duke. But to what purpose is not expounded.

A month later he wrote from near Heidelberg:

> We marched here in twenty days. The troops are in a very good condition, having been very well supplied with forage…and the girls much handsomer than we expected to find in this country.

On 2 July the Anglo-Dutch army forced a crossing of the Danube in the bloody storming of the Schellenberg strongpoint. The cavalry carried fascines for the infantry and then went forward to rally them after they were twice repulsed. The third assault was successful and the cavalry were unleashed on the fleeing Bavarians.

On 13 August the allied armies under Marlborough and Prince Eugene faced the French and Bavarian armies at the small village of Blindheim – always Blenheim to the British – by the Danube. Repeated allied infantry and cavalry attacks pinned the French in position and weakened their centre, enabling Marlborough to launch his massed cavalry in a decisive action. The French

The capture of the standard of the Bavarian Horse Guards by the 5th Dragoon Guards at Elixhem, 18 July 1705. (RDG)

cavalry broke and fled the field, suffering huge losses. British records are incomplete but the 5th (present in squadron strength) lost one officer killed and the 7th lost four officers and probably had up to 50 casualties.

The victory at Blenheim ended the threat to Vienna and marked the start of Britain's ascent to global power. It was the first battle honour awarded to the parent regiments of the Royal Dragoon Guards.

The following year the war reverted to Flanders. Feinting skilfully, Marlborough forced a crossing of the fortified Lines of Brabant at dawn on 18 July 1705 with the seizure of river crossings at Elixhem. The British cavalry, 16 squadrons in all, rapidly crossed, formed into line and soon found themselves facing some 40 French and Bavarian squadrons. Marlborough personally led the charge in which the 5th, riding in the centre, overwhelmed the Bavarian Household Cavalry and captured four of their standards. In less than two hours Marlborough had pierced the vaunted French fortifications, utterly routed the enemy cavalry and taken over 3,000 prisoners. In his dispatch he wrote: 'Amongst the Horse Brigadier Cadogan's Regiment [the 5th] had the honour to charge first…'

The brilliant action at Elixhem was unique in Marlborough's campaigning as it was essentially a cavalry fight. However, strangely it was never granted as a battle honour.

The success at Elixhem could not be exploited due to differences with Marlborough's Dutch allies, who in the following month also refused to support an attack at Waterloo. The next major battle took place at Ramillies in May 1706. It was a resounding victory in which the 5th and 7th joined in the final pursuit.

A prolonged lull followed, and it was not until July 1708 that the armies clashed again in the encounter battle of Oudenarde where only nightfall saved the French from complete destruction. The battle was preceded by a rapid overnight march during which the British cavalry seized the river crossing at Lessines, where the 7th would fight again in 1918 and, post-amalgamation, 1940. The cavalry then covered the siege of Lille and the 5th fought at Wynendael, where the French unsuccessfully attempted to intercept a major supply convoy.

By 1709 the allies held most of Flanders and directly threatened France. On 11 September Marlborough's army assaulted a well-defended French position at Malplaquet. The 5th and 7th were heavily engaged in the greatest clash of cavalry yet seen in Europe. The French eventually retreated but the allies were fought to a standstill in the bloodiest battle of the war.

The French refused to end the war and constructed vast defensive works in northern France – the *Non Plus Ultra* lines – running along much of the future Western Front. In August 1711 Marlborough used a series of rapid marches and feints to bluff the French and force the lines close to Cambrai. The British cavalry formed the advance guard and a troop of the 5th nearly captured the French commander-in-chief, who narrowly escaped despite the loss of his escort.

The war finally ended in 1713. In ten long years of campaigning the British Army had shattered the myth of French invincibility and become feared and respected across Europe.

WAR OF THE AUSTRIAN SUCCESSION, 1742–48

In 1742 the 7th and the 6th (Inniskilling) Dragoons joined a British expeditionary force in another anti-French alliance. In June 1743 King George II took command of an Anglo-German army in an attempt to secure Hanover. On 27 June he was nearly caught in a trap at Dettingen by a stronger French force. Lacking room for manoeuvre, tactical skill mattered less than sheer hard fighting. Mustering only 180 effectives, the 7th took part in an unsuccessful counter-attack to support the hard-pressed British infantry, one of whom wrote:

> [the 7th] was surrounded and overpowered, and forced to fight their way back through the enemy, as the only means of preventing their being totally cut off.

Cornet Richardson defending the Standard of the 7th Dragoon Guards during the battle of Dettingen, 27 June 1743. (RDG)

Cornet Henry Richardson was wounded 37 times while protecting the regimental Standard but brought it to safety. Despite having lost a third of its strength, the 7th reformed and charged again with their brigade, as part of a general allied advance that led to the French line collapsing. The infantry witness recalled:

The 7th Dragoon Guards at the battle of Dettingen, 27 June 1743. (RDG)

> I came behind [the 7th] and saw an old veteran corporal and half a dozen comrades who had fought through the enemy; and covered with wounds: he addressed his companions while observing their present wretched condition – that they had begun the day well, and hoped they would end it so; and collecting their small squadron of heroes, they recharged the thickest of the enemy.

Dettingen was the last occasion in which a British monarch commanded his army in action. There was no more fighting in Germany and the army returned to Flanders, going into winter quarters at Lessines. The 7th and the Inniskillings fought at the battle of Fontenoy in 1745 where the allied army was defeated. The Inniskillings also fought at Rocoux in 1746 and at Lauffeld in 1747, where they took part in a desperate charge to cover the retreat of the allied infantry, suffering some 120 casualties.

SEVEN YEARS' WAR, 1756–63
This was the first global war, fought across continents and oceans. In 1758 the Inniskillings' newly raised light troop took part in raids on the French coast, burning shipping and stores.

The main campaigning took place in northern Germany where a British expeditionary force was again deployed to defend Hanover against French invasion. When not in the field, the 7th and Inniskillings went into winter quarters in Münster, Osnabrück and Paderborn – places their armoured successors would come to know well after 1945.

The Inniskillings were present at Minden in 1759 when the commander of the British cavalry failed to support the infantry and was subsequently court-martialled and dismissed. The cavalry, including the Inniskillings and the 7th, made amends the following year when under bolder command they decisively routed the French cavalry at Warburg.

FRENCH REVOLUTIONARY WAR, 1793–95

In 1793 a small British expeditionary force, including the 5th and the Inniskillings, attempted to clear French revolutionary armies from Flanders. At Beaumont in 1794 the army was surprised in fog by a larger French army, but the fog lifted to show the French left flank was open. A covered outflanking movement by the allied cavalry, including the 5th, brought them undetected into the French rear. Their surprise was complete and the French were routed.

Two weeks later the Inniskillings helped to break French squares at Willems in another successful cavalry action. However, subsequent allied defeats forced the British force to fall back into Holland. The campaign ended disastrously with the army retreating into Germany in appalling winter conditions. The Inniskillings formed part of the rearguard and fought off several French attacks.

CHAPTER SIX – MAJOR WARS OF THE 19TH CENTURY

NAPOLEONIC WARS, 1811–15

The Peninsula and France, 1811–14

In 1807 Napoleon invaded Spain and Portugal. He placed his brother, Joseph, on the Spanish throne the following year, resulting in a popular revolt. A British expeditionary force under Sir John Moore entered Spain to help the anti-French insurgents. However, facing Napoleon's concentrated armies, Moore was forced to retreat in the depths of winter to Corunna where his army was evacuated.

Another British force landed in Lisbon in 1809 under command of General Arthur Wellesley (the future Duke of Wellington). By 1811 he had liberated Portugal and that summer he received reinforcements, including the 4th and 5th Dragoon Guards.

The fall of the frontier fortresses of Badajoz and Ciudad Rodrigo in early 1812 opened the way for Wellington to advance into Spain. In April the 5th led Le Marchant's cavalry brigade in a 60-mile forced march that surprised a French cavalry brigade at Llerena. Charging twice, the brigade scattered the French and pursued them for four miles. Curiously, no battle honour or campaign medal clasp was awarded for the cavalry action at Llerena as the troops had not been engaged by musket fire.

Three months later, with the two armies manoeuvring in close proximity at Salamanca, Wellington spotted that the French had over-extended their left wing and immediately attacked. Le Marchant's brigade, led by the 5th, made a series of devastating charges and in 30 minutes the brigade defeated eight French battalions and helped wreck the French left wing, at the cost of barely a hundred casualties including the brigade commander who was killed in the final stages. The 5th captured the staff of the drum-major of the 66th Regiment, known today as the Salamanca Staff and carried on regimental parades.

Madrid fell to Wellington but French counter-moves threatened his communications and he was forced to withdraw to the Portuguese frontier. The retreat was conducted in great hardship, exacerbated by torrential rain and the failure of the supply system. Sickness ravaged the troops and horses died in appalling numbers from exhaustion and want of forage. Fortunately, the retreat was largely unhindered by the equally exhausted French.

The shortage of horses reduced the British cavalry to crisis point. The 4th, which could only find 89 troop horses for 311 men, was one of five cavalry regiments ordered to hand over their horses to other regiments and were then sent back to Britain, missing the final phase of the campaign.

In May 1813 the army advanced once again into Spain. The French made an unsuccessful stand at Vittoria, where huge quantities of supplies, treasure and money were plundered by Wellington's army. The 5th managed to avoid the Duke's wrath at this widespread breakdown of discipline.

Vittoria opened the way into France over the Pyrenees. The mountainous terrain was unsuited for the use of cavalry on any scale and it was not used until the following spring when Wellington drove the French back to Toulouse, where the 5th was part of the advance guard. Paris fell to the allied offensive from the east and Napoleon abdicated in early April. However, the news took a week to reach the southern front, where the 5th took part in the last great battle of the campaign at Toulouse.

Waterloo, 1815

Napoleon was exiled to the Mediterranean island of Elba, but escaped to France in early 1815 and raised a new army, which included many of his veterans. Allied armies were rapidly mobilised to oppose him. Wellington took command of an Anglo-Dutch-Belgian army in the Low Countries, with a Prussian army under Blücher close by. The British troops included the 6th (Inniskilling) Dragoons as part of the Union Brigade, which also comprised the Royal Dragoons and the Scots Greys. Wellington's army included a core of Peninsular veterans, but many of his troops were raw and inexperienced and the loyalty of the Belgians was in doubt.

The Inniskilling Dragoons in leaguer the night before Waterloo, 17–18 June 1815. (RDG)

Wellington and Blücher agreed to combine forces south of Brussels, but Napoleon moved more swiftly than anticipated. On 16 June he attacked the Prussians at Ligny and a second force under Marshal Ney attacked Wellington's covering position at the vital crossroads at Quatre Bras, nine miles south of Waterloo. Wellington's infantry fought resolutely and, despite heavy casualties at Ligny, the Prussians withdrew in good order towards Wavre, where Blücher could still support Wellington. The British cavalry, which had been widely dispersed for better access to forage, spent the day marching towards the battlefield. That night the Union Brigade, after a difficult march of 50 miles along heavily congested roads, bivouacked at Genappe, just north of Quatre Bras.

The forced withdrawal by the Prussians made Wellington's situation untenable, and on 17 June he withdrew to a pre-planned position astride the Brussels road just south of Waterloo. The cavalry covered the withdrawal and the Inniskillings provided three troops to help carry wounded infantry. That night Wellington's army took up position on the reverse slope of a low ridge astride the Brussels road. The torrential rain that fell all night was seen as a good omen by veterans who remembered a similar downpour prior to Salamanca. The Household and Union brigades were in the centre behind the main infantry positions, which were anchored by the strongpoints at Hougoumont chateau on the right and La Haye Sainte in the centre. That night Wellington was assured by his Prussian liaison officer that Blücher would march to his support in the coming battle.

Napoleon opened the battle of Waterloo on 18 June with a diversionary attack on Hougoumont and a major artillery bombardment. These were the preliminaries to the main attack in the centre by massed French infantry columns reinforced by cavalry. The brunt of the attack fell on the British infantry in the centre who poured volley fire into the French and then counter-attacked. The Household and Union brigades charged in support, with the Inniskillings and Royals in the first line of the Union Brigade. They rode into and through the French infantry before colliding with the French cavalry 'like the meeting of two stone walls'. The British cavalry drove the French down the slope and pushed forward towards the French batteries, having smashed an infantry corps and part of its cavalry. However, the British regiments became widely scattered and their hard-worked horses were exhausted. The commander of the Union Brigade (Brigadier Ponsonby, late of the 5th) was killed trying to rally his troops, and both the Union and Household brigades were extricated with difficulty under concentrated French cavalry attack and heavy artillery fire. The depleted Union Brigade, under command of its only surviving commanding officer, Lt Col Muter of the Inniskillings, fell back into reserve.

Napoleon now launched his cavalry in a series of prolonged but costly attacks against the unbroken squares of British infantry. At 6pm La Haye Sainte fell when its defenders ran out of ammunition, a counter-attack failed and a dangerous gap opened in the allied line. At this critical point of the battle the Union Brigade was deployed in a single line to make the force appear stronger than it was. They were under fire from artillery and skirmishers, which was described by one officer as 'the most trying duty of the day'.

Napoleon launched the Imperial Guard in a desperate last attempt at victory even as Prussian troops began to arrive on his right flank, but the French columns were beaten back by sustained British infantry fire. At 8pm Wellington signalled the general advance and the French retreat became a rout.

Wellington's army was utterly exhausted and the Prussians took up the pursuit of Napoleon's fleeing army. The Inniskillings had started the day 397 strong but by nightfall could muster barely two hundred. The commanding officer and second in command were badly injured in the final stages and the senior captain brought the regiment out of action.

Waterloo was a searing battle, the name of which is forever associated with decisive victory. Every soldier who fought there received a sum of prize money equivalent to six weeks' pay, was credited with two years' service towards his pension and was listed on nominal rolls as a 'Waterloo Man'. A figure of an Inniskilling Dragoon is one of the four sentinels at the base of the statue of the Duke of Wellington at Hyde Park Corner.

CRIMEAN WAR, 1854–56

In 1853 tensions between Russia and Turkey spilled into war. Britain and France agreed to support Turkey with armed intervention and declared war on Russia in 1854. Allied forces assembled at Varna in Bulgaria to prepare for an assault on the Crimea and the important naval base at Sevastopol. The 4th and 5th Dragoon Guards and the 6th (Inniskilling) Dragoons,

The departure of the 4th Dragoon Guards for the Crimea, 1854. (RDG)

together with the Royals and the Scots Greys, were in the Heavy Brigade commanded by Brigadier General Scarlett (late of the 5th). Together with the Light Brigade it formed the Cavalry Division commanded by Lord Lucan. The British force was commanded by the elderly Lord Raglan. Nearly half a century of peace and stagnant leadership meant the army was in a poor state and wholly unprepared for war. Its shortcomings in command, training and administration would be mercilessly exposed during the campaign.

The Inniskillings suffered a severe setback before arriving in the Crimea when the troop ship *Europa*, carrying their regimental headquarters, caught fire a day after sailing from Plymouth. When invited to move to another part of the ship for his own safety, the commanding officer replied: 'I see none of my men there and I will not leave them.' He was one of 14 Inniskillings who died, along with all the horses.

The cavalry initially disembarked at Varna, where deadly cholera rapidly broke out in the badly sited and unhealthy camps. Equine diseases were also rampant. The inadequacies of the supply and medical services that were to bedevil the early stages of the war became swiftly apparent. Shortages were exacerbated by a huge fire that destroyed valuable stores including boots and rations.

In September the expeditionary force began to land unopposed in the Crimea. The Heavy Brigade landed at Balaklava and went into camp on the plain beyond the port. It had missed the Battle of the Alma, where failure to exploit the allied victory gave the Russians time to reinforce the defences of Sevastopol.

The bombardment of Sevastopol finally began on 17 October. The Cavalry Division remained in front of Balaklava as part of the small force defending the vital British base and only link to the outside world. On 25 October a Russian sortie from Sevastopol led to the famous actions of the Battle of Balaklava.

The Battle of Balaklava

The battle took place over two valleys divided by a ridge known as the Causeway Heights. The Cavalry Division was camped to the west of the south valley and routinely stood to before dawn on 25 October. The Heavy Brigade's ten weak squadrons totalled some 800 men. Just after first light a large Russian force assaulted Turkish redoubts on the Heights. The Turks held out for over an hour before abandoning their positions. The Cavalry Division had moved forward in support but came under artillery fire and was controversially ordered by Lord Raglan, from his commanding position overlooking both valleys, to withdraw west towards their camps.

It was now nearly 10am and the early mist had cleared. From his distant vantage point Lord Raglan saw a massed force of Russian cavalry advancing unopposed along the north valley. The Cavalry Division had barely returned to the west end of the south valley before Lord Lucan was ordered to send eight squadrons of the Heavy Brigade back towards Balaklava. General Scarlett led his brigade eastwards in an open column of troops, the Inniskillings leading followed by the Greys and the 5th, with the 4th echeloned further back. Neither the Heavy Brigade nor the approaching Russian cavalry had scouts out or were aware of their proximity to each other. The ground in the south valley was difficult, with vineyards obstructing the path of the squadrons and forcing the leading regiments into two parallel columns.

Suddenly, Scarlett's ADC saw Russian cavalry silhouetted on the skyline of the Heights. Scarlett immediately ordered the Inniskillings, Greys and 5th to left wheel into line. The much larger Russian force also wheeled into line and deployed flanking wings. However, they then halted some 400 yards away. Scarlett ordered his trumpeter to sound the charge and led off.

The first Inniskilling squadron and the Greys crashed into the Russian mass just behind Scarlett. The Russian wings began to close in from both flanks and the remaining British squadrons came successively into action within a few moments of each other. The 5th charged from the left rear of the Greys as they were being enveloped by the Russians. Troop Sergeant Major Franks of the 5th wrote:

The charge of the Heavy Brigade at Balaklava on 25 October 1854 by Major Elliott. The 5th Dragoon Guards are shown moving through the Light Brigade camp. (UK Ministry of Defence © Crown Copyright)

OVERLEAF: The Inniskilling Dragoons charging with the Heavy Brigade at Balaklava on 25 October 1854. (Courtesy of the Council of the National Army Museum, London)

It was rather hot work for a few minutes; there was no time to look around you. We soon became a struggling mass of half-frenzied desperate men, doing our best to kill each other.

The second Inniskilling squadron struck the Russian left wing as it was wheeling inwards. The 4th seized the initiative as Scarlett had done and, switching swiftly from column to line, slammed into the disorganised Russian right wing. The charges of the 4th and the second Inniskilling squadron were decisive and after just eight minutes the Russians withdrew in disorder over the Heights.

Poor personal relationships between the British commanders, indecision and sheer incompetence meant that the Light Brigade failed to support the Heavy Brigade charge or attack the fleeing Russians, who were therefore able to retire to the far end of the north valley. Lord Raglan's subsequent muddled orders that afternoon resulted in the Light Brigade's heroic but costly charge against Russian guns in the north valley. The Heavy Brigade advanced in support of the Light Brigade, but was ordered to retreat having come under heavy fire from artillery on the Heights. Troop Sergeant Major Franks recalled:

We could see through the smoke the dim outline of the Light Brigade galloping towards the thirty-six field pieces that stretched across the plain, and as we were proceeding at a rapid pace, we soon got under fire also. Some of our men and horses were knocked over before we had got fire, and in a few minutes we were in the direct line of fire, the shot and shell ploughing up the ground around us.

The charge of the Heavy Brigade at Balaklava on 25 October 1854. (RDG)

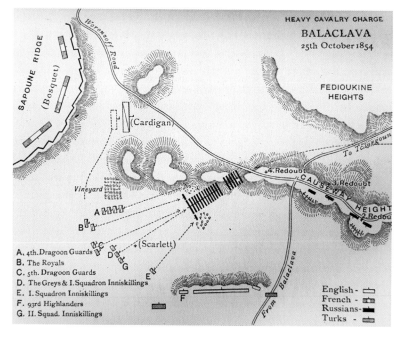

HEAVY CAVALRY CHARGE
BALACLAVA
25th October 1854

FEDIOUKINE HEIGHTS

A. 4th. Dragoon Guards
B. The Royals
C. 5th. Dragoon Guards
D. The Greys & I. Squadron Inniskillings
E. I. Squadron Inniskillings
F. 93rd Highlanders
G. II. Squad. Inniskillings

English -
French -
Russians -
Turks -

The Heavy Brigade's casualties for the day were surprisingly light, with ten killed and 98 wounded. More than half the 5th's casualties were incurred while supporting the Light Brigade.

The charges of both brigades established a formidable reputation for the British cavalry. Such was the effect on the Russian cavalry that they kept their distance for the rest of the war. Almost a year of siege operations followed before Sevastopol fell in September 1855 and a formal peace was concluded.

Soldiers of the 4th Dragoon Guards with French soldiers and Mrs Rogers, wife of an NCO of the 4th, during the Crimean War. Mrs Rogers acted as a cook and laundress for the regiment and was admired for her bravery. (Courtesy of the Council of the National Army Museum, London)

CHAPTER SEVEN – THE FIRST WORLD WAR, 1914–18

The First World War was fought in Europe, Africa, the Middle East, across the world's oceans and, for the first time, in the air. The war's defining theatre was the Western Front which, following the initial clashes, was formed of trenches and fortifications running from the Belgian coast through northern France to Switzerland. The founding regiments of the Royal Dragoon Guards fought exclusively on the Western Front and spent the entire war in France and Flanders with the British Expeditionary Force (BEF).

FRANCE AND FLANDERS, 1914

Germany invaded Belgium on 3 August 1914. Britain declared war the following day and the BEF – two corps and a cavalry division that included the 4th and 5th Dragoon Guards – immediately mobilised and deployed to France. Both regiments deployed at war strength of some 550 all ranks with 600 horses, organised in three sabre squadrons and a machine-gun section. Reservists from regiments stationed in India reinforced the BEF, including a number of Inniskilling Dragoons attached to the Life Guards.

The BEF extended the French left flank to meet the anticipated German thrust through Belgium. The cavalry covered the BEF's move into Belgium and within days both regiments were in contact with the enemy. Early on 22 August, C Squadron of the 4th encountered a German cavalry patrol near the village of Casteau, just north of Mons. Two troops under Captain Hornby charged, and 1st Troop had a brief skirmish in Casteau, wounding one

German and capturing several more. The Germans fell back and were joined by reinforcements. The soldiers of 4th Troop dismounted and Corporal Thomas fired the first British shot of the war in Europe. After a brief firefight the Germans withdrew, pursued by both troops. Private Tilney, Hornby's orderly, remembered:

> I followed the Captain as he went down the road. He took a German on the point of his sword, just as I saw the lads do at Shornecliffe with the dummies. I took on a German with a lance, whom I captured.

C Squadron now came under fire from more German cavalry and their supporting infantry. Learning from prisoners that they were facing the lead elements of a German cavalry division, the squadron withdrew unhindered to Casteau, taking with it five prisoners and without suffering a single casualty.

This and subsequent contacts, together with aerial reconnaissance reports, confirmed that two advancing German armies threatened the flanks of the BEF and their neighbouring French formation. The successful delaying action at Mons on 23 August saw the famed rapid fire of the British infantry, but German strength was growing swiftly and the BEF was forced to withdraw. The 4th took part in a critical flank guard action against a German corps at Audregnies on 24 August, which included an ill-conceived charge that cost the regiment 81 casualties. Private Clouting of C Squadron recalled:

> All around me men and horses were brought hurtling to the ground amidst fountains of earth. Ahead, the leading troops were caught up by agricultural barbed wire, so that horses were beginning to be pulled up when I heard for the one and only time in the war a bugle sounding 'troops right wheel'. I pulled my horse round, then with a crash, down she went.

The regiment was momentarily fragmented but regained its cohesion over the next few days as many soldiers originally reported as casualties straggled in.

The cavalry covered the BEF's infantry during the retreat from Mons. This involved occasional skirmishes and long, exhausting days in the saddle in intense heat. The regimental diary of the 4th for the first week of September recorded:

1.9.14   Received orders to be ready to march at 4.30am
2.9.14   Orders received at 2am to turn out as quickly as possible
3.9.14   Marched at 4.20am
4.9.14   Ditto
5.9.14   Marched 5am

Shortly after first light on 1 September the 5th were feeding their horses with the rest of their brigade at the village of Nery, when they were surprised in thick mist by a German cavalry division.

Responding rapidly, the brigade commander ordered the 5th to turn the German right flank. So many horses had been scattered by German shelling that the regiment could only mount two squadrons. Leaving C Squadron and the machine guns in support, the commanding officer led A and B squadrons out of the village. Despite coming under heavy fire they dismounted and opened fire with deadly effect, particularly against the Germans' led horses.

This bold and audacious action, greatly aided by the mist, which was still thick in places, stopped the attack of two German cavalry regiments and secured the northern flank, enabling the brigade to regain the initiative. The Germans withdrew in disarray, abandoning most of their artillery. Among the 20 casualties incurred by the 5th was the commanding officer. Mortally wounded, his dying order to his soldiers who carried him back to cover was that they should return at once to the firing line.

Although a small action that was not officially awarded as a battle honour, Nery damaged the German cavalry so much that it failed to detect a newly formed French army that menaced the German open right flank as it pursued the BEF and French armies to the southeast of Paris.

On 6 September the French launched a major counter-attack on the Marne. The BEF, led by the cavalry, advanced into a wide gap between two German armies, with the 4th and 5th fighting in a series of encounter actions against rearguard actions. By early October fighting became deadlocked on the river Aisne and the features of trench warfare began to emerge.

The BEF then moved to Flanders as part of the 'race to the sea' to cover the hundred miles of open flank from the Aisne battlefield to the coast. Fighting centred on the town of Ypres, which was critical to the defence of the Channel ports. The BEF was soon entrenching and in action against German armies advancing in strength.

Sergeant Slaughter MM and Private Keys of the 4th Dragoon Guards in trenches at Bethune, winter 1915–16. (RDG)

The 4th and 5th were almost continuously in action throughout the First Battle of Ypres. At the crisis of the battle at the end of October they fought dismounted, in trenches and buildings on the Messines–Wytschaete ridge, against the sustained onslaught of two Germans corps supported by heavy artillery. The two regiments suffered a combined 110 casualties before coming out of the line.

The German offensive was finally brought to a standstill on 22 November and the long stalemate of the trenches began. The cavalry was gradually withdrawn from the lines to form a mobile reserve and the 4th and 5th spent the rest of the year settling into the routine of the front. This involved tours in the primitive trenches in icy conditions, but they were mostly billeted in farms and villages, building horse shelters and frequently standing-to.

Training started, reinforcements arrived and warm winter clothing was issued. Home leave began and games flourished, especially football. Welfare parcels trickled in and on Christmas day every soldier received a Christmas card and gift box from Princess Mary.

The Indian Cavalry Corps, including the 7th Dragoon Guards and the Inniskillings, landed at Marseilles in mid-October. Following a short period of acclimatisation and the exchange of tropical dress for winter kit, they moved to the front. The 7th had a grim baptism of fire on 20 December when their commanding officer was mortally wounded in a counter-attack to recover some lost trenches at Festubert. This action cost the regiment 41 casualties.

FRANCE AND FLANDERS, 1915

Renewed fighting came in the spring. In April the Germans attacked using gas at Ypres and dismounted British cavalry went into action in what became the Second Battle of Ypres. The 4th and 5th were continuously in the trenches for a fortnight in May and each regiment suffered over one hundred casualties, including the commanding officer of the 5th, who was wounded.

The rest of 1915 saw increasing frustration for the mounted arm, with occasional spells in the line, endless pioneer tasks, training and standing by for the elusive breakthrough. In December a composite division of dismounted cavalry was formed for service in the trenches for which the 4th and 5th provided company-sized detachments.

BELOW: The 7th Dragoon Guards and the Deccan Horse, on the Western Front, 1916. (RDG)

FRANCE AND FLANDERS, 1916

A major British-led offensive was planned on the Western Front as part of a series of allied offensives. The cavalry earnestly hoped that their turn would come in the expected breakthrough and a 'striking force' was formed for this purpose. Designated cavalry routes were constructed and specialist trench bridges were designed to enable mobility.

The Battle of the Somme began on 1 July with appalling casualties. A second major assault began a fortnight later, and on 14 July the Secunderabad Cavalry Brigade, including the 7th and the Deccan Horse, was ordered to support infantry attacks against the commanding position of High Wood.

Cheered by infantrymen and gunners, the 7th led the first cavalry advance since the beginning of trench warfare. B Squadron, armed with lances, deployed at a gallop and successfully charged German machine-gunners sheltering in shell holes. As enemy fire became intense, the squadron dismounted and went into action with rifles and machine guns. It subsequently withdrew, having lost three killed and 21 wounded.

Although the British assault petered out with little gain, much was made of the charge by the press. However, while the offensive continued until November, there was no chance of exploitation by the cavalry. In September Captain Wright of the 4th wrote: 'They say caterpillar forts [tanks] are being used for the first time. They should be a great success.'

Stagnation set in again for the rest of the year. Each regiment had to find 265 soldiers for stints in a pioneer battalion, laying light railways and building roads. This resulted in additional work for the remaining soldiers, who had to care for all the horses.

FRANCE AND FLANDERS, 1917

In March the Germans began withdrawing from the Somme to the formidable defences of the Hindenburg Line. Another British offensive began in April, with some gains at Vimy and Arras, where the 5th were involved in some sharp fighting, but no real progress was made.

The cavalry spent the greater part of 1917 in monotonous spells of training and fatigues far behind the front, interspersed with detachments being sent to the trenches. Life was occasionally enlivened by patrols and raids; in July three troops of the 7th mounted a raid that inflicted several German casualties and the Inniskillings carried out a successful raid on a German strong point.

Following the end of the Third Battle of Ypres in November, another offensive was launched at Cambrai. The initial assault on 20 November – led by nine battalions of tanks, many crewed by former cavalrymen – achieved complete surprise and inflicted heavy casualties. Five cavalry divisions were concentrated in readiness to exploit these initial successes.

The 4th, closely followed by the 5th, moved forward at the head of their division to seize crossings on the St Quentin Canal. However, progress was slowed by the shell-torn ground, trenches and uncleared wire. The 4th, 5th and 7th fought some bold troop and squadron actions along the canal, but loss of momentum due to communications breakdowns and stiffening German resistance led to the advance stalling. The only cavalry to actually make a breakthrough was A Squadron of the 4th. Approaching the edge of Cambrai, the squadron charged a column of horse transport and infantry, capturing some 50 prisoners and two ammunition wagons before being forced to withdraw at a cost of 14 casualties, including the squadron leader.

The 4th Dragoon Guards moving up at Cambrai, November 1917. (RDG)

By 24 November all chance of a breakthrough had gone. The 5th had spent nearly three days in the saddle, fought two engagements and marched over 50 miles. The Germans launched a major counter-attack on 30 November and the 4th, 5th and 7th left their horses to reinforce the infantry. On 1 December the Inniskillings were ordered to seize a ridge at Villers-Guislain. C Squadron, forming a flank guard, captured a German trench but was pinned down and extricated with difficulty. The remainder of the regiment advanced unsupported into heavy machine-gun fire. D Squadron, in the lead, pressed on for some two miles. It reached the cover of a beet factory but came under heavy artillery fire before being surrounded by German infantry; the survivors were taken prisoner. The commanding officer immediately withdrew the other two squadrons. This fiasco cost the Inniskillings 114 casualties and the machine-gun section was a total loss.

By early December the high hopes of Cambrai had been dashed and the cavalry resumed the tedious routine of dismounted reliefs and working parties during the fourth winter of the war.

FRANCE AND FLANDERS, 1918

The start of 1918 saw a major restructuring of the cavalry, with the 7th and Inniskillings leaving their parent Indian brigades. The Germans launched an enormous offensive against the BEF on 21 March in an attempt to force a final decision. In desperate fighting the cavalry was used to plug gaps across the front, extricate exhausted infantry and cover flanks. Regiments were in almost continuous action until early April, with the 7th suffering 73 casualties, mainly from shellfire. The Germans were finally fought to a standstill in front of the vital road and rail hub of Amiens, but a further series of German offensives were launched across the Western Front over the next three months.

The tide finally turned at Amiens on 8 August with a major British attack in which all four regiments participated. The terrain was well-suited to cavalry and tanks, and rapid progress was made. The 5th were the first regiment to reach the final objective line at Harbonnières, where it captured a troop train that was attempting to flee. The regimental 'bag' for the day also included 760 prisoners, three field guns, several trucks and wagons and a number of horses. It had covered over six and a half miles in under six hours at a cost of seven killed and 62 wounded. One squadron leader noted that many men 'had to be detached for prisoner escort duty, destroying material, searching headquarters for important documents...'

The Inniskilling Service Squadron

At the outbreak of war in 1914 a service squadron of the Inniskillings was formed from the cavalry of the Ulster Volunteer Force and a cadre of regular Inniskilling instructors. It arrived in France in September 1915 and was used as divisional and corps cavalry, including at the Somme. In 1917, in response to the need for more infantry, the squadron was dismounted and became B Company of the 9th Battalion Royal Irish Fusiliers. It fought at Bourlon Wood during the German counter-attack at Cambrai, at the Battle of the Lys in 1918 and in the final advance to victory.

OVERLEAF: The 5th Dragoon Guards' A Squadron capturing a German train at Harbonnières, 8 August 1918. (RDG)

A Squadron of the 7th Dragoon Guards seizing the bridge at Lessines minutes before the Armistice came into effect, 11 November 1918. (RDG)

8 August 1918 became known as the 'Black Day of the German Army' and was the start of the Allied advance that continued into the autumn.

ARMISTICE

Early on 11 November troops received a message that hostilities would cease at 11am. At 9.35am, A Squadron of the 7th, detached as divisional cavalry,

Casualties

Of the 551 members of the 4th Dragoon Guards who landed in France in 1914, 359 became casualties. Eighty-four were killed in action or died of wounds or illness. A further 199 were wounded, 27 on two or more occasions, and 76 were taken prisoner of war. These figures exclude those who were transferred to other regiments during the war, of whom at least four were killed.

was ordered to seize the river crossings at Lessines, some ten miles away, before the armistice came into effect. The squadron immediately saddled up and galloped forward, picking up a detached troop and dealing with some German machine-gunners en route. By 10.45am they had captured the village, secured the bridge, which had been prepared for demolition, and taken some 160 prisoners.

On 1 December the cavalry crossed the frontier into Germany and on 12 December the 4th were the first British troops to cross the Rhine. All four regiments remained with the army of occupation until 1919.

CHAPTER EIGHT – THE SECOND WORLD WAR, 1939–45

Following the First World War there were severe cutbacks to the army. In 1922, the 4th and the 7th were amalgamated, as were the 5th and the Inniskillings. After the appalling human cost of the war, Britain and France sought to avoid military confrontation in the 1930s, and the new regiments were not mechanised until 1938 on the eve of the next war. Limited numbers of light tanks and carriers were issued for their new role as divisional reconnaissance regiments. Hitler invaded Poland on 1 September 1939 and Britain declared war two days later.

FRANCE AND BELGIUM, 1939–40

Both regiments arrived in France in September 1939 with the new BEF. While Poland was overrun, the new Western Front was left almost entirely alone for some eight months of 'phoney war'. This gave vital time for badly needed training, interrupted by occasional alerts.

The French and British planned to advance into Belgium and conduct a forward defence to counter any German advance. However, Belgium's insistence on neutrality until actual German aggression prevented preliminary moves across the border. Germany planned to hold the Allies in Belgium and envelop them with a move through northern France to take the Channel ports, cutting off the BEF's escape route.

Germany invaded Belgium on 10 May 1940 and the BEF moved some 80 miles to take up positions on the river Dyle. Both regiments screened the river crossings while the infantry dug in and the 4th/7th linked up with French troops on their right flank. From 11 May, the roads began to fill with refugees and then columns of retreating

Belgian soldiers. On 14 May A Squadron of the 4th/7th clashed with a German reconnaissance group of motorcyclists and armoured cars. Both sides sustained casualties, but as German pressure mounted the British screen withdrew.

The German breakthrough at Sedan led the French to give way and forced a general withdrawal. The Skins found themselves on a disintegrating boundary with inadequate command arrangements. They came under vigorous attack and their neighbouring regiment, the 15th/19th Hussars, was surrounded and overrun. The Skins took the survivors under command and withdrew across the river Dendre.

On 19 May the 4th/7th fought a delaying action on the Dendre against a strong German attack. Fighting was particularly fierce at Lessines, the site of the final action by the 7th Dragoon Guards in 1918. The regiment withdrew in contact, losing a complete troop in an ambush. It regrouped having lost over a third of its vehicles and suffering 25 casualties, but having enabled the infantry to withdraw according to plan.

By 23 May both regiments were back in France and the gravity of the situation facing the BEF became clear. Despite a partially successful counter-attack by the BEF's armour at Arras on 21 May, Panzer forces had broken through the Allied front and were driving on the Channel ports. Under relentless pressure a wide gap opened between the BEF and the French front. Both regiments were tasked again with supporting infantry withdrawing in

The Phoney War: the commanding officer of the 4th/7th Royal Dragoon Guards briefs his squadron leaders in the Pas-de-Calais, October 1939. (Imperial War Museum)

contact, and clashed several times with German advance guards. By now they were severely reduced in vehicle strength and reorganised to form two composite groups. The first comprised a mounted squadron from the 4th/7th and two from the Skins. The second comprised the dismounted crewmen from both regiments and the 15th/19th Hussars.

The BEF's front was narrowing into a bridgehead, and on 26 May the evacuation from Dunkirk began under heavy Luftwaffe attacks and scenes of chaos. All heavy equipment and vehicles were to be destroyed and soldiers would be taken off from the beaches or the harbour. The dismounted group reached Dunkirk on 29 May and were evacuated the following day. The mounted squadrons fought off German attacks in rearguard actions under increasing pressure as roads were mined and bridges blown. On 1 June they broke contact and withdrew to Dunkirk. After wrecking their vehicles and spending an uncomfortable day on the beach under intermittent shelling and air attack, they were evacuated that night. The enduring legacy of the campaign was the tactical recognition flash adopted by the 4th/7th and worn today on the Royal Dragoon Guards service dress.

The Missing Tank

On 15 May a tank from C Squadron of the 4th/7th broke down near the river Dyle. By the time its driver, Lance Corporal Ablot, got it going again his squadron, and the regiment, had disappeared. Despairing of locating either, Ablot navigated himself across Belgium and France to Calais. He arrived just ahead of the Germans and embarked with the tank on one of the last ships to leave. It was the only BEF light tank to return to Britain.

THE LONG WAIT, JUNE 1940–JUNE 1944

Both regiments were initially concentrated at Bovington with little more than their personal weapons. The threat of invasion was high and the army was in poor shape after the disaster in France. Equipment was woefully inadequate or non-existent, and reconstitution was to be a long, slow process. Victory in the Battle of Britain spared the nation from invasion, but neither regiment could imagine it would be four long years before they saw action again. They were subjected to a succession of moves, reorganisations, reequipping and retraining, which never seemed to bring them nearer active service. There were continued demands for drafts to reinforce regiments in the Middle East, and many volunteered for operational service. Both regiments provided 69 men each as the nucleus of the 22nd Dragoons, a wartime-only regiment.

In early 1943 the 4th/7th were detailed for the assault force that would open the long-awaited 'Second Front' in Europe – Operation OVERLORD. The regiment joined 79th Armoured Division, which was developing specialised armoured vehicles and techniques for beach landings and assaults on fortified positions. The 4th/7th converted to amphibious tanks, which could swim ashore under their own power to provide close support to the

The years of waiting nearly over; soldiers of the 4th/7th Royal Dragoon Guards resting at Southampton before embarking for D-Day. (RDG)

infantry in the first minutes of an assault. Buoyancy came from a rubberised canvas screen attached to the hull, which had to be collapsed swiftly for the tank to come into action. Two propellers were powered by Duplex Drive (DD) and a tiller provided sluggish steering. Intensive training began, initially in great secrecy, on converted Valentine tanks, then Shermans. The canvas screen was easily damaged and in rough weather there was a severe risk of swamping. Crewmen wore an escape apparatus and survival training culminated in an escape from a mock-up flooded tank hull.

The 4th/7th practised launching from Landing Craft Tanks (LCTs) off the Isle of Wight, followed by intensive training with the landing force on the Moray Firth. Further training took place on the south coast, but tragedy struck on 4 April 1944 when six tanks were swamped by heavy seas off Studland Bay and sank with the loss of six soldiers.

The Skins spent 1942 to 1944 training intensively as an armoured regiment, latterly on the new Cromwell tank. Frustration increased as their parent division was omitted from the order of battle for the Normandy landings and there was no news of any other operational role. Indeed, as D-Day approached the division began to be broken up amid looming fears that its regiments might remain inactive at home or be used to provide individual reinforcements. Finally, on 10 July 1944, over a month after D-Day, the Skins were warned to move to Normandy.

NORMANDY ASSAULT AND BRIDGEHEAD, 1944

Each assaulting infantry brigade/regimental combat team on the five beaches of the Allied landings would be backed by an armoured regiment/battalion of DD tanks. At Gold Beach on the British western flank the 4th/7th would support an infantry brigade with two DD squadrons. A third squadron, equipped with Firefly Shermans, fitted with 17-pounder guns, would wade ashore from LCTs. After saturation air and naval bombardment the swimming squadrons would land with the infantry, subdue any initial resistance and then advance inland.

Echelon vehicles of the 4th/7th Royal Dragoon Guards embarking at Southampton, June 1944. (RDG)

The 4th/7th left the Solent on the morning of 5 June, adverse weather having postponed D-Day by 24 hours to 6 June. The following morning the sea was calmer, but conditions were too rough at 0635, launch hour. The LCTs, therefore, closed on the beach for H-Hour at 0725. Trooper Baker was in the C Squadron armoured recovery vehicle:

> There were destroyers right in close to the beach, firing like mad: they must have been almost aground. Rocket ships and SP [self-propelled] guns firing from LCTs added to the general racket.
>
> There was a tremendous crash and the LCT jerked backwards: it had hit a mine... the ramp was damaged, but went down ok.

There was little serious resistance during the actual landing, although five tanks were swamped or mined on the beach. The regiment pushed inland but resistance stiffened in close country, with casualties inflicted by a well-sited 88mm anti-tank gun and friendly fire from naval shelling. The 4th/7th leaguered six miles inland near Creully, having suffered 12 killed and 18 wounded and lost 19 tanks. The assault force was now ashore and a lodgement secured.

A Sherman tank in the Normandy bocage. (Imperial War Museum)

BREAKOUT FROM NORMANDY

The weeks following D-Day saw bitter fighting to expand the bridgehead. Although the Allies had air and artillery superiority, German opposition was formidable, aided as it was by the bocage country – a maze of small orchards and fields enclosed by thick, banked hedgerows, intersected by narrow sunken lanes, which was ideal for defence. The 4th/7th were continuously engaged for six weeks, with squadrons supporting infantry in a series of fierce actions resulting in a steady flow of casualties. B Squadron was reduced to a single

Two of the five German Panther tanks knocked out by Sergeant Harris and his gunner, Trooper Mackillop, of A Squadron of the 4th/7th Royal Dragoon Guards at Lingèvres, 14 June 1944. Sergeant Harris was awarded the Distinguished Conduct Medal for this action. (Imperial War Museum)

tank on 11 June at Cristot. On 14 June a Sherman Firefly of A Squadron knocked out five German Panthers at Lingèvres. Trooper Baker, now a Sherman operator, was in action on 26 June when C Squadron lost six tanks:

> I was munching boiled sweets by the dozen and the others were smoking furiously. Suddenly the tank behind us was hit. I saw a spout of earth shoot up beside it as a shot ricocheted into it. Smoke curled up from the turret…

By late July the 4th/7th had suffered 125 casualties. However, British and Canadian attacks had forced the Germans to concentrate their Panzer divisions in the east of the Normandy bridgehead. This enabled the US armies to break out in the west in Operation COBRA on 25 July.

The Skins began active operations on 2 August in a major offensive to secure Mont Pincon as the front began to expand. By the middle of the month the remnants of the German forces in Normandy were encircled at Falaise. Both regiments regrouped for the next move, which began on 20 August with the advance east towards the Seine. Although the Germans were far from collapse, the situation became more fluid with rapid advances

Cromwell tanks of the 5th Royal Inniskilling Dragoon Guards entering Lisieux, 21 August 1944. (RDG)

German prisoners of war with soldiers of the 5th Royal Inniskilling Dragoon Guards, Normandy, August 1944. (RDG)

and joyful welcomes from liberated civilians. Leading tanks of the 4th/7th crossed the Seine on rafts on 26 August as the Battle of Normandy ended.

ADVANCE TO THE FRONTIERS

The Germans were now in full retreat and the Allies were advancing on a broad front. The 4th/7th, now in an independent armoured brigade, set off at speed on 30 August, covering up to thirty miles a day with occasional skirmishes against individual enemy tanks or self-propelled guns. The Skins crossed the Seine on 31 August and advanced to Amiens. Both regiments now passed through country familiar from 1940. The 4th/7th entered Lille amid wild celebrations on 3 September and crossed the Belgian border the following day. The Skins reached Ghent on 6 September, having covered 250 miles in six days.

Both regiments were in action as the advance continued towards the Dutch border. Supply lines had become over-extended and flanks were vulnerable. A German counter-attack along the Albert Canal hit the brigade echelon, costing the 4th/7th a dozen ammunition and fuel trucks. In mid-September the advance paused to allow time for maintenance and for reinforcements and supplies to catch up.

Both regiments played minor roles in Operation MARKET GARDEN, the attempt by airborne and ground forces to secure river and canal crossings up to the Rhine at Arnhem. On 20 September the 4th/7th recced an alternative route north of Nijmegen. B Squadron linked up with Polish paratroopers at Driel but attempts to cross the Rhine failed and the British airborne forces were withdrawn. The Skins were tasked to reopen the supply corridor north of Eindhoven. They saw three days of sharp fighting alongside American paratroopers before the road was cleared.

Sherman tanks of the 4th/7th Royal Dragoon Guards entering the Dutch village of Weert, September 1944. (Imperial War Museum)

There was now a supply crisis, making it essential to clear the approaches to the port of Antwerp. The Skins were, therefore, detached to support an infantry division tasked with capturing the strongly held town of 's-Hertogenbosch. The attack began on 22 October across heathland interspersed with hamlets and woodland, which was made hazardous for tanks by drainage ditches and patches of bog. Progress was slow, but tank/infantry teams, reinforced by specialist armour, fought their way into the town, which was secured on 24 October.

WINTER CAMPAIGN AND FINAL ROUND

At the end of October both regiments were able to have a brief spell of rest and local leave, and undertake much-needed maintenance. The respite for the 4th/7th was broken in early November at Geilenkirchen where they supported an American attack on the Siegfried Line. Offensive operations were suspended until January when both regiments took part in the fighting to clear the west bank of the Rhine. They then withdrew to prepare for the final phase of the war. The plan was for the Anglo-US armies to cross the Rhine, envelop the Ruhr industrial region and thrust across Germany to meet the Russians on the Elbe.

The 4th/7th crossed the Rhine on 24/25 March, followed two days later by the Skins. Both regiments then advanced rapidly, but had several tough battles while clearing towns and villages

Second World War Campaigns

4th/7th Royal Dragoon Guards and
5th Royal Inniskilling Dragoon Guards
  North-West Europe 1940, 1944–45

Principal Battle Honours

4th/7th Royal Dragoon Guards
  Dyle
  Dunkirk 1940
  Normandy Landing
  Odon
  Mont Pincon
  Nederrijn
  Geilenkirchen
  Rhineland
  Cleve
  Rhine
5th Royal Inniskilling Dragoon Guards
  Withdrawal to Escaut
  St Omer-La Bassee
  Dunkirk 1940
  Mont Pincon
  Lower Maas
  Roer

A Sherman tank of C Squadron of the 4th/7th Royal Dragoon Guards with infantry in the Reichswald, February 1945. (RDG)

against fierce German opposition. Trooper Baker's tank was hit by an 88mm round and panzerfaust on 28 March:

> The welded track plates were all smashed and scattered. Low down by the suspension was a neat hole made by the bazooka. The blast seemed to have gone under the turret floor. The inside of the tank was a shambles and it was lucky for us we had bailed out when we did.

The 4th/7th crossed the Weser on 15 April and reached Bremen on 25 April. There was hard fighting against pockets of last-ditch resistance from German paratroopers and Waffen-SS before the city was secured.

The Skins had a difficult action at Ibbenbüren on 3/4 April, suffering 16 casualties while fighting skilful German instructors and cadets from an infantry school. They crossed the Weser on 14 April and began the final stages of the advance to the Elbe against a disintegrating enemy.

Germany surrendered unconditionally on 7 May and the following day was celebrated as VE (Victory in Europe) Day. When news of the German surrender was received, the 4th/7th were approaching Bremerhaven and the Skins had reached the Kiel Canal.

Casualties

In the 11 months from D-Day the 4th/7th lost 127 soldiers killed, 189 wounded and 22 taken prisoner. In the same period the regiment lost 93 tanks destroyed and 48 damaged beyond first-line repair. The Skins lost 57 soldiers killed and 152 wounded.

CHAPTER NINE – THE COLD WAR

At the end of the Second World War Germany was divided into four occupation zones by the Allied powers. In 1949 the three western zones merged to form the Federal Republic of Germany and the Soviet zone in the east became the German Democratic Republic. In the same year the North Atlantic Treaty Organisation (NATO) was founded, and in 1955, after West Germany was admitted to NATO, the Soviet Union responded with its own military alliance in central and eastern Europe, the Warsaw Pact. The breakdown of relationships between the former allies led to the 'Cold War', a state of armed confrontation that did not end until the fall of the Berlin Wall in 1989.

KOREAN WAR, 1951–52

The Cold War periodically erupted into conflict, most dangerously in Korea. In 1945, following Japan's surrender, the Korean peninsula was split into communist North Korea and pro-western South Korea. The uneasy truce between them ended abruptly in June 1950 when North Korea invaded the south in the hope of achieving swift victory before international intervention.

The United Nations Security Council authorised and requested armed assistance to South Korea. Britain was swift to respond, with troops and warships in action within days. An American-led counter-offensive swept into North Korea, resulting in Chinese intervention at the onset of winter. The UN forces were forced to retreat, but by spring 1951 the front had stabilised on the 38th Parallel, with the tactical situation akin to the trench warfare of 1914–18.

The 5th Royal Inniskilling Dragoon Guards deployed to Korea in December 1951 to form part of the 1st Commonwealth Division. The terrain was a mix of mountains and deep narrow valleys of small paddy fields divided by bunds. Winters were severe, with temperatures of minus 30°C recorded in February 1952, and consequently tanks had to be started every two hours. Summers were hot, wet and humid with monsoon conditions that swept away roads and bridges.

Tank troops were deployed within infantry company positions on high ground forward of the river Imjin, providing pinpoint direct fire support.

A Centurion main battle tank of the 5th Royal Inniskilling Dragoon Guards crossing the River Imjin, Korea, summer 1952. (RDG)

A Centurion main battle tank of the 5th Royal Inniskilling Dragoon Guards with its crew, Korea, summer 1952. (Imperial War Museum)

Crews lived beside their tanks, originally in tents and bashas, then in dugouts as enemy shelling and mortaring increased. Squadrons rotated through a month in the line followed by a month in reserve.

Although truce talks had begun, the front line was increasingly active. On the night of 5 April 1952, the regimental headquarters tanks and 3rd Troop C Squadron assisted their neighbouring infantry in repulsing a battalion-size probe. The tanks fired nearly four hundred rounds of 20-pounder high explosive. Although more intense than usual, this was typical of many nights on the line.

As the weather improved, the pace of operations quickened. Tanks supported large infantry fighting patrols and squadrons participated in mobile raids with British, Australian and Canadian infantry. A major regimental raid, Operation JEHU, took place against Chinese positions on 17 June. Three tanks were bogged while withdrawing and their recovery became a complex operation with infantry, engineer and artillery support. The final tank was not recovered until 25 June.

Enemy artillery fire intensified against forward tank positions during the summer. Despite overhead protection, on 5 September a Centurion suffered

A Centurion main battle tank of A Squadron of the 5th Royal Inniskilling Dragoon Guards on Hill 210, Korea, winter 1952. (RDG)

a direct hit in the turret, which killed the crew. Heavy shelling of Point 159 resulted in one troop leader's tank being replaced twice in a fortnight, with damage from 30 hits in total.

Although the war was very static, the threat of being overwhelmed by mass Chinese assaults was ever present. In early November 1952 4th Troop B Squadron was deployed with the Black Watch to defend a vital feature known as the Hook, a ridgeline that dominated no-man's land and the Imjin river crossings. On the night of 18/19 November heavy shelling was followed by a major Chinese attack. The troop was deployed at both ends of the ridge and brought down heavy fire on the attackers, using tank searchlights to illuminate targets until they were obscured by smoke or damaged by shrapnel. The initial Chinese attack overran the forward company before being driven off. A subsequent Chinese attack was launched and overran the Hook again. The troop leader moved his tank onto the narrow ridge to support the Black Watch counter-attack, but the tank was set on fire by a rocket and the driver was wounded. At first light a Canadian counter-attack finally secured the Hook and the troop withdrew to harbour positions. It had been engaged for nine hours and fired 144 rounds of 20-pounder high explosive and thousands of rounds of machine-gun ammunition.

The regiment suffered 13 killed and 27 wounded in a year on the line in Korea. It was the first campaign in which wounded were often evacuated by helicopter, enabling rapid treatment and increased survival rates.

BRITISH ARMY OF THE RHINE

Throughout the Cold War there were only eight years when neither of the regiments were stationed in West Germany on the front line. Regiments always had to be at a certain minimum strength and were always at notice

A Chieftain main battle tank and Stalwart amphibious vehicle of the 5th Royal Inniskilling Dragoon Guards, Hohne ranges, West Germany, c.1977. (RDG)

Chieftain main battle tanks of B Squadron of the 5th Royal Inniskilling Dragoon Guards at the Brandenburg Gate, Berlin, autumn 1976. (RDG)

to deploy to wartime positions. Periodic exercises tested recall and deployment procedures as well as the evacuation of families.

Operational plans assumed 1st British Corps holding a defensive line on the river Weser against the most likely axis for a Warsaw Pact offensive. In 1961 the Berlin Wall went up and the possibility of the Cold War becoming an armed conflict was very real.

Both regiments usually served in armoured roles with main battle tanks. At first the principal equipment was the Centurion, initially with 20-pounder guns, later with the 105mm. In the 1950s one troop per squadron was equipped with the heavy Conqueror tank with a 120mm gun. Chieftains and their 120mm guns arrived in the late 1960s/early 1970s, as did the FV438 fitted with Swingfire anti-tank guided missiles. For a short time in the 1960s regiments had their own air squadrons of up to six helicopters, which were subsequently absorbed into the Army Air Corps.

A Scorpion CVR(T) of the 4th/7th Royal Dragoon Guards on exercise in West Germany in the 1980s. (RDG)

The large training areas and ranges previously used by the Wehrmacht were requisitioned and large-scale exercises took place, usually in the autumn months. After 1954, manoeuvre rights had to be granted by the West German authorities under the Schedule 443 system and compensation was paid for damage to crops, roads and fences. Other than these major exercises, armoured training was restricted to training areas such as Soltau and the gunnery ranges at Hohne. A major facility was established in 1972 in Canada, which provided considerably more scope for realistic live-fire manoeuvre training than was possible in Germany.

The annual training cycle began with winter, which was largely devoted to individual training. Troop and squadron training took place in the spring, followed by major divisional – and occasionally corps – exercises in the summer and autumn. Gunnery camp was an annual fixture and regimental headquarters was also involved in command post exercises to test planning and procedures. The year was interspersed with other tasks and activities such as site guards and adventure training, including skiing in Bavaria. There were also occasional patrols of the Inner German Border, largely in order to fly the flag. Both sides viewed each other silently across the fence but no recognition or fraternisation was permitted.

Gunnery was a skill that ranked high for armoured regiments in West Germany. The Canadian Army Trophy was an annual competition to foster excellence among NATO armoured units, with Belgium, Canada, the United Kingdom, the Netherlands, the United States and West Germany taking part. In 1979 the 4th/7th Royal Dragoon Guards represented the British Army and came third.

The British brigade in West Berlin included an armoured squadron, a role both regiments carried out in the 1970s and 1980s. There was also an annual requirement to relieve the resident squadron to carry out troop training and gunnery in West Germany. C Squadron of the 5th Royal Inniskilling Dragoon Guards was the last squadron from either regiment to carry out this enjoyable commitment in the summer of 1988, the year before the Berlin Wall fell.

END OF THE COLD WAR AND AMALGAMATION

The Cold War ended dramatically with the fall of the Berlin Wall in November 1989 and the subsequent collapse of the Warsaw Pact and the Soviet Union. This triggered a defence review and a substantial reduction in size of the British Army. With many other regiments, the 4th/7th and Skins paid the price of the 'Peace Dividend'. Seventy years after both regiments were formed, they came together as the Royal Dragoon Guards.

Both regiments were stationed in the newly unified Germany when the amalgamation was announced. The 4th/7th were at Detmold and the Skins at Paderborn, where they had been based originally in 1948. On 1 August 1992 they paraded formally at Paderborn as the Royal Dragoon Guards, a new armoured regiment in the British Army's order of battle. The Prince of Wales became the regiment's Colonel-in-Chief, and HRH The Duchess of Kent its Colonel Duchess.

CHAPTER TEN – 21ST-CENTURY OPERATIONS

The century opened with the Royal Dragoon Guards stationed at Münster in Germany and converting to the Challenger 2 main battle tank. The regiment was on Exercise SAIF SAREAA in Oman in September 2001 when Al-Qaeda launched its attacks on the Twin Towers in New York and the Pentagon in Washington. The attacks opened an era of wars and insurgencies in Afghanistan and Iraq. These complex campaigns dominated regimental life for over a decade and saw soldiers operating on main battle tanks and also in a host of new roles.

IRAQ, 2004–08

In 2003 Saddam Hussein's regime was swiftly overthrown by an American-led coalition. However, the coalition found itself occupying a traumatised and divided state with weak or ineffective institutions, crumbling infrastructure, a brewing insurgency and increasing sectarian violence.

The Royal Dragoon Guards deployed across southern Iraq on Operation TELIC 5 in late 2004. Regimental headquarters, HQ, B and C squadrons were based at the old RAF airfield at Shaibah, initially conducting security and escort tasks and providing an armoured reserve. A Squadron formed part of an infantry battlegroup based at Al-Amarah in Maysan province, operating both with armour and in the light role. The situation was fragile, with occasional ambushes and indirect fire attacks by Shia insurgents, and inter-tribal fighting north of Basra.

In early 2005 the regiment was re-tasked to form a battlegroup with an area of operations from the Kuwait border to the edge of Basra city. This included the town of Az Zubayr, ports, communication routes, oil

The Royal Dragoon Guards battlegroup headquarters in the 'Qurna Elbow', north of Basra, during Operation TELIC 11. (RDG)

infrastructure and sensitive coalition facilities. B Squadron covered the Al-Faw peninsula, including a strategic oil pumping station. C Squadron was responsible for the ports of Umm Qasr and Khor Al Zubair and the border crossing at Safwan. An early task for the regimental battlegroup, along with all coalition forces, was providing security for Iraq's first democratic elections in January 2005. Work also began to help the embryonic Iraqi security forces towards self-reliance.

The regiment returned to Iraq in late 2007 for Operation TELIC 11. There were frequent changes in organisation and tasking up to, and during, the deployment, and additional vehicle conversion requirements placed extra demands on the regiment during work-up training.

The situation in southern Iraq had deteriorated significantly since 2005, with British troops suffering rising casualties from Iranian-backed Shia militias using increasingly lethal improvised explosive devices (IEDs). Indirect fire attacks were also increasing, particularly against the main British base at Basra Airport. The regiment deployed as the brigade operations battlegroup, with A and C squadrons in Warrior and Bulldog armoured fighting vehicles respectively. B Squadron provided the UK armoured force as part of the divisional reserve battlegroup, and D Squadron formed part of a mentoring and training battlegroup.

The regimental battlegroup operated in Basra and Maysan provinces, conducting long-range ground and air manoeuvre operations. Extended lines of communication meant that resupply, including engines and spares, was by helicopter. B Squadron's tanks led every operation by the divisional reserve battlegroup. The squadron also directly supported Iraqi and multinational force strike operations in Basra city against determined opposition including multiple IED strikes. D Squadron deployed into the centre of Basra city at short notice in April 2008 in order to facilitate and mentor Iraqi Army operations during Operation Charge of the Knights – an

D Squadron of the Royal Dragoon Guards operating Warrior armoured fighting vehicles at night in Basra during Operation TELIC 11. (RDG)

Iraqi-led operation to re-establish control over the city. This was a demanding role, conducted in austere conditions, and two of its Warrior fighting vehicles were disabled by enemy action. Several of the regiment's soldiers were wounded, but there were no fatalities.

AFGHANISTAN, 2010–13

Following the attacks on 11 September 2001 ('9/11') the United States led an international coalition in operations against Taliban and al-Qaeda bases in Afghanistan. The Taliban were swept from power and an interim government was formed by Hamid Karzai. The International Security and Assistance Force (ISAF) was set up to maintain security in Kabul and its surrounding areas. Taliban remnants withdrew to southern Afghanistan and the Pakistan tribal areas. In 2006 ISAF's role was extended to all provinces, but its focus became the emerging insurgency in the south, particularly in Helmand and Kandahar provinces.

The Royal Dragoon Guards deployed on Operation HERRICK 12 in summer 2010. The regiment was spread widely throughout southern Afghanistan, from Sangin in northern Helmand, through Gereshk in the centre, to Nad-e Ali in the south, as well as Kandahar city some 80 miles to the east of Helmand. B Squadron provided protected mobility in support of three infantry battlegroups. C Squadron was in a ground-holding infantry role. D Squadron formed the Viking Group, a mobile force giving fire support to infantry battlegroups under pressure across the brigade area. Reconnaissance Troop, based in Kandahar, provided protected mobility for the British general commanding all ISAF troops in southern Afghanistan. In addition, some 80 soldiers were employed in other roles, with 11 in the Brigade Reconnaissance Force and the remainder as forward air controllers, police mentors, liaison officers and staff officers. The climate was

Soldiers of D Squadron of the Royal Dragoon Guards on patrol in the Green Zone on the River Helmand during Operation HERRICK 17. The regimental tactical recognition flash is clearly visible. (RDG)

unforgiving, with extreme summer temperatures requiring herculean feats of endurance, particularly while operating dismounted with helmet, body armour and personal loads.

Soldiers performed almost every function within the military spectrum as they took part in operations to protect the local population, spread influence, secure progress and push the Taliban out of their former strongholds. These operations involved combat against a cunning and skilful enemy who was not afraid to take on ISAF troops with rocket-propelled grenades, small arms and fiendish IEDs. Four soldiers were killed in action, the regiment's first operational deaths since it was formed in 1992, and over 30 were wounded in action, some severely. However, close comradeship and the best possible medical support for the wounded ensured that morale remained high.

Every day on Operation HERRICK 12 required resilience, determination and courage, particularly in the face of the ever-present IED threat. Nonetheless, the regiment was able to witness tangible progress being made, with locals returning to their former homes, shops and businesses opening and local Afghan governance taking hold in areas where the Taliban once ruled by fear.

Two years later the regiment returned to Helmand on Operation HERRICK 17 as the Police Mentoring Advisory Group (PMAG) with a large number of attached soldiers, including a Danish contingent, under regimental command. The deployment phase was complicated and it took over two and a half months before the regiment was complete on the ground. There had been much progress in Afghanistan since Operation HERRICK 12. The population was more secure, the insurgents were under pressure and the Afghan Army was more professional and more confident. The Afghan police, however, suffered from corruption and needed significant support and training.

PMAG headquarters was based at Lashkar Gah, with Headquarters Squadron running Afghan police training at the Lashkar Gah Training Centre. B, C and D squadrons provided advisory and mentoring teams to Afghan security forces across central Helmand, and D Squadron also advised the Helmand Operations Coordination Centre. Finally, A Squadron formed the Warthog Group providing protected mobility and fire support across the brigade area of operations.

The tour saw a rapid pace of change. Soldiers initially mentored Afghan patrolmen on checkpoints and in the precincts. By the end of the tour light mentoring touches were provided at the highest level, and very few soldiers were deployed on the ground as the Afghan police became increasingly independent, confident and competent.

Soldiering in Afghanistan remained dangerous and challenging. Small teams of soldiers lived and worked alongside Afghan forces, often in isolated locations. As well as the reduced, but still potent, Taliban threat, they faced the ever-present risk of 'Green on Blue' insider attacks by disaffected Afghan soldiers and police. The regiment had no fatalities, but one soldier was seriously wounded supporting an Afghan National Police operation.

OVERLEAF: Corporal Bainbridge rescuing a wounded soldier under enemy fire in Helmand, Afghanistan, in 2013. He was awarded the Military Cross for gallantry in this and a series of other actions against the Taliban during Operation HERRICK 17. (RDG)

Soldiers of the Royal Dragoon Guards and Afghan National Police at a vehicle checkpoint, Helmand, Operation HERRICK 17. (RDG)

THE FUTURE

It would be fruitless to make any predictions about what the future might hold for the Royal Dragoon Guards. However, recent campaigns have been undertaken with adaptability, flexibility, quickness of thought and action and good-humoured determination. These attributes were inherited from their forebears, of whom they have proved themselves worthy successors. We may be confident that the regiment and its soldiers will meet future challenges in a similar manner.

Corporal Carter of the Royal Dragoon Guards leading an endurance march on Pen-y-Fan in the Brecon Beacons, 2018. (UK Ministry of Defence © Crown Copyright)

APPENDICES

Appendix A – Operational Gallantry Awards

Key (with dates instituted):

CGC – Conspicuous Gallantry Cross (1993)
DCM – Distinguished Conduct Medal (1854 – replaced by the CGC from 1993)
DSO – Distinguished Service Order (1886)
MC – Military Cross (1914 – incorporated the MM from 1993)
MM – Military Medal (1916 – absorbed into the MC from 1993)
QGM – Queen's Gallantry Medal (1974)
VC – Victoria Cross (1856)

Crimea 1854–55
4th Dragoon Guards
DCM   8

5th Dragoon Guards
DCM   8

6th (Inniskilling) Dragoons
DCM   8

Sudan 1884–85
4th Dragoon Guards
DCM   3

5th Dragoon Guards
DCM   2

The Boer War 1899–1902
4th Dragoon Guards
DCM   1

5th Dragoon Guards
VC   Lieutenant John Norwood
DSO   1
DCM   2

6th (Inniskilling) Dragoons
DSO   2
DCM   8

7th Dragoon Guards
DSO   3
DCM   5

First World War 1914–18
4th Dragoon Guards
DSO   11
MC   17
DCM   4 (records incomplete)
MM   9 (records incomplete)

5th Dragoon Guards
DSO   4
MC   14
DCM   19
MM   31

6th (Inniskilling) Dragoons
DSO   3
MC   10
DCM   12 (records incomplete)
MM   40 (records incomplete)

7th Dragoon Guards
DSO   15
MC   21
DCM   11
MM   48

Second World War 1939–45
4th/7th Royal Dragoon Guards
DSO   4
MC   17
DCM   2
MM   20

5th Royal Inniskilling Dragoon Guards
DSO   8
MC   21
DCM   7
MM   23

Palestine 1946–48
4th/7th Royal Dragoon Guards
MC   1

The Korean War 1951–52
5th Royal Inniskilling Dragoon Guards
MC   3
MM   1

South Arabia 1965–66
4th/7th Royal Dragoon Guards
MM   1

Northern Ireland 1972–99
4th/7th Royal Dragoon Guards
MC   2
QGM   1

Iraq 2004–08
Royal Dragoon Guards
MC   1

Afghanistan 2010–13
Royal Dragoon Guards
MC   2

APPENDIX B – COLONELS-IN-CHIEF[1]

5th Dragoon Guards	1915–22	HM Albert I, King of the Belgians
7th Dragoon Guards	1914–22	HRH The Duchess of Fife
6th (Inniskilling) Dragoons	1898–1922	HRH The Duke of Connaught
4th/7th Royal Dragoon Guards	1922–31	HRH The Duchess of Fife
	1977–92	HRH The Duchess of Kent
5th Royal Inniskilling Dragoon Guards	1922–34	HM Albert I, King of the Belgians
	1937–83	HM Leopold III, King of the Belgians
	1985–92	HRH The Prince of Wales
Royal Dragoon Guards	1992–	HRH The Prince of Wales
	1992–	HRH The Duchess of Kent, The Colonel Duchess

APPENDIX C – AFFILIATIONS AND ALLIANCES

Royal Navy
HMS *Daring*

Royal Air Force
XI Squadron

Affiliations
A (Yorkshire Yeomanry) Squadron, The Queen's Own Yeomanry
C (Cheshire Yeomanry) Squadron, The Queen's Own Yeomanry
B (North Irish Horse) Squadron, The Scottish and North Irish Yeomanry

Allied and Affiliated Regiments

The Fort Garry Horse – a Canadian reserve reconnaissance regiment whose history ranges from subduing the Canadian West to fighting in both world wars.

The British Columbia Dragoons – a Canadian reserve reconnaissance regiment that fought in both world wars.

The 4th/19th Prince of Wales Light Horse – an Australian reserve light cavalry regiment, originally raised in 1914, which fought at Gallipoli, on the Western Front and in Palestine during the First World War.

The Queen Alexandra's Mounted Rifles – a New Zealand armoured cavalry regiment, originally raised in 1864, whose history includes service in the Maori wars, the Boer War and both world wars.

The 15th Lancers (Baloch) – a Pakistani cavalry regiment formed in 1922 by the amalgamation of the 17th Cavalry and the 37th Lancers (Baluch Horse).

The Deccan Horse – an Indian cavalry regiment that can trace its roots to 1790. It fought alongside the 7th Dragoon Guards on the Western Front.

The 12e Regiment de Cuirassiers – a French cavalry regiment originally raised in 1688. It fought in the Napoleonic wars, including at Waterloo, and in both world wars. More recently, it saw active service in Mali and Lebanon.

---

1 The 4th Dragoon Guards never had a Colonel-in-Chief.

BIBLIOGRAPHY

The 4th/7th Royal Dragoon Guards

Brereton, J. M., *A History of the 4th/7th Royal Dragoon Guards*, published privately, Catterick (1982)

d'Avigdor-Goldsmith, Maj J. A., *Short History of the 4th, 7th and 4th/7th Royal Dragoon Guards*, Gale & Polden, Aldershot (1943)

The 5th Royal Inniskilling Dragoon Guards

Blacker, Gen C.and Evans, Maj Gen R., *Change and Challenge: 5th Royal Inniskilling Dragoon Guards*, Spottiswoode Ballentyne Press, London (1978)

Evans, Maj-Gen R., *The 5th Royal Inniskilling Dragoon Guards*, Gale & Polden, Aldershot (1951)

Jackson, Maj E. S., *The Inniskilling Dragoons*, Arthur L. Humphreys, London (1909)

Pomeroy, Maj R. L., *History of the Fifth Dragoon Guards*, Blackwood, Edinburgh (1924)

INDEX

References to images are in *italics*.